The Essence of Aikido

By Bill Sosa and Bryan Robbins

UP UNIQUE
PUBLICATIONS

Edited by Sandra Segal and Dave Cater
Designed by Danilo Silverio and Nancy Hara–Isa

UNIQUE PUBLICATIONS
4201 Vanowen Place
Burbank, CA 91505

ISBN: 0-86568-097-3
Library of Congress Catalog Card Number: 87-50404

Please note that the publisher of this instructional book is NOT RESPONSIBLE in any manner whatsoever for any injury which may occur by reading and/or following the instructions herein.

It is essential that before following any of the activities, physical or otherwise, herein described, the reader or readers should first consult his or her physician for advice on whether or not the reader or readers should embark on the physical activity described herein. Since the physical activities described herein may be too sophisticated in nature, it is ESSENTIAL THAT A PHYSICIAN BE CONSULTED.

The Essence of Aikido

Table of Contents

stances—30

" Extension of Ki—74

To the founder of aikido, Master Morihei Ueshiba

Foreword

As a young freshman in college, I became fascinated by the art of judo when introduced to it by a good friend who was a devotee of the ancient Japanese art form. Somehow it seemed appropriate to be banged around the mats while attempting to apply various strangling, holding, throwing and joint-bending techniques or waza. As other interests became more important, judo fell by the wayside and the martial arts were not to be encountered again until, as a 35-year-old professor of marketing, I was introduced to karate by one of the authors (Bryan Robbins) of this book. Karate was exhilarating but as I advanced up the ranks, it became apparent that the still young but aging body was not willing to tolerate the punishment necessary for continuing advancement. After having been absent from the martial arts for a couple of years, it was the same Bryan Robbins who convinced me that he had come upon the ultimate in martial arts and one that would be most suitable for my needs. With some mild apprehension, I began my venture into aikido.

Introduction

aikido, one of the youngest and least well-known of the martial arts, has been labeled the non-violent or loving martial art. For those familiar with the martial arts, these labels seem a contradiction of terms. Images of ear-shattering screams and painful kicks, punches and throws immediately rush to the minds of those familiar with the more famous martial arts of karate, judo, jujutsu, kung-fu and many others. It is difficult to imagine a martial art that focuses on rendering an opponent helpless with such a loving attitude that your very opponent does indeed become helpless without the expense of serious (or any) physical injury. Indeed, the only injury may very well be to the ego of that unknowing opponent foolish enough to attack a well-trained aikidoist. Even more difficult to comprehend is the notion that "less is more" in the relationship between the *nage* (the one being attacked) and the *uke* (the attacker). That is, the more forceful the attacker, the less energy that is needed to be expended by the one being attacked.

While these concepts are difficult to envision in the mind that is more accustomed to clashing with opponents in every conceivable way (physically, mentally, emotionally, competitively and so forth) rather than harmonizing or blending with an opponent, it is the mission of this book to convince the reader that the theories and concepts of aikido are most applicable in everyday life to everyone interested in leading a more harmonizing life, regardless of lifestyle. The reader will quickly learn that this loving art is more than a course in self-defense; rather it is a course in the approach to leading a life that is potentially free from the constant conflict of clashing with one's self as well as with both significant and insignificant others that must be dealt with on a daily basis. While it is true that the vast majority of these pages are devoted to physical techniques, it is the philosophy of aikido and its spirit of harmony and blending with one's environment that leap from the pages of this book.

The Essence of Aikido is a technique-oriented treatment of the art of aikido. The book is ladened with approximately 450 professional photographs of the authors illustrating scores of techniques that emphasize the dramatic variety of aikido. The photographs help the reader to analyze and break down the finesse of these many techniques. It is said that there are more than 10,000 techniques in aikido and it is a life-long learning process. Nevertheless, with just a few lessons in aikido, most beginning students immediately grasp its vast potential for enriching their lives. To be sure, however, the reader cannot learn by only reading; but it is a beginning. Those who find the philosophy and explanations of the techniques provided in this book as interesting and exciting as they are, would do well to begin training as early as possible. Only then can the many opportunities of applying aikido in everyday life begin to be realized. For those who have already begun training or are teachers of aikido, this book will be most helpful in the continuation of that fascinating training and teaching leading to the harmony and peace in life that the vast majority of us seek.

THOMAS E. BARRY, Ph.D.
Professor of Marketing
Edwin L. Cox School of Business
Southern Methodist University
Dallas, Texas

Acknowledgements

The authors' attitude is not that they are the highest authorities on the subject of aikido, but merely a wish to share with other people what limited knowledge we may have. It is believed that one must empty the cup before it is refilled.

At the same time it is only proper that we pay tribute to the aikido teachers who started us on the path.

Bill Sosa particularly wishes to thank Isao Takahashi, his first aikido teacher who believed in him and encouraged him to teach when teaching was the last thing on his mind. A very patient, gentle and caring man who appreciated and taught the art of aikido accordingly.

Koichi Tohei, who more than any one man is responsible for bringing aikido to America and other parts of the world.

Roy Suenaka, whose friendship, time and energy were not wasted, but rather appreciated.

His thanks also goes to Shihan Rod Kobayashi, Chief Instructor and founder of Seidokan Aikido in Los Angeles, California, whose efforts have been to teach aikido to the American public in a manner best suited to the American culture, whereas its utilization is not used solely as a means of self-defense but more significantly as something that is applicable to our daily life. His gratitude and many thanks goes to Kobayashi sensei for helping him all these years to better understand aikido. He would also like to thank Bryan Robbins, his co-author and good friend, for all his help in putting this book together and for taking all those falls in the picture-taking sessions.

Bryan Robbins would like to express his appreciation to his martial arts instructors — Keith Yates and Bill Sosa. These men have been excellent examples of the benefits of martial arts training. Thanks also to Shirley Baker for typing the manuscript. Finally he wishes to acknowledge his parents, Florence and Bill Robbins, for being the greatest supporters of his athletic and academic endeavors.

*Morei
Ueshiba*

Today's world is filled with violence and adversity. Many people feel that through violence and suppression our enemies can be broken and eliminated. Instead of showing love and compassion to our fellow man, we show our muscle (nuclear arms, weapons of war and weapons of the street) and refuse to truly sit and talk to each other. The question of humanity is when will we learn to harmonize (*aiki*) with one another and stop the eternal fighting. When will we learn to blend with nature and quit our constant destruction and pollution of our planet? Many people from all over the world feel that aikido is the most suited martial art of our age.

Master Ueshiba, founder of aikido, concluded that the purpose of martial arts was the perfection of the spirit, not merely perfection of physical technique. Although the modern forms of budo, such as kendo, karate and judo, stress the importance of mind-body training, they also emphasize competition and tournaments and therefore place an emphasis on winning. It is at this juncture that aikido shows itself to be unique. Aikido holds no tournaments or contests and refuses competition as it is detrimental to progress on the spiritual path. The temptation always to be a winner would lead people to be egotistical and self-centered and develop a win-at-all-costs attitude. Defeating others was seen as a roadblock in the path to harmony in the universe.

Students of aikido are constantly reminded to let go of the "fighting mind." Care is taken during actual practice to avoid clashing against another person's energy. When the student feels that he is forcing a technique, it is a sure sign he is clashing with his partner's energy instead of blending or going around the force. Using brute strength in aikido is a sign of failure to execute technique properly. Only after years of practice does one truly recognize that it is unimportant to see who is the best, who is the strongest, who is the champion. The true path of budo is the path toward spiritual enlightenment. Training in aikido has no end; perfection of character is never complete.

Practice at an aikido dojo is held in a helpful and harmonious atmosphere. There is no rivalry because no one wins or loses. Students are instructed to maintain the idea of harmony and non-aggression in their daily lives.

"Winning means winning over the discord in yourself. Those who have a warped mind, a mind of discord, have been defeated from the beginning."

— *Morihei Ueshiba*

14

History and Philosophy

Morihei Ueshiba, the founder of aikido, was born Dec. 14, 1883. During his early childhood, he was rather sickly and weak. Despite this and because of his fascination with the esoteric Buddhist rites, by the age of eight he began learning the Chinese classics under the direction of a Shingon priest and thought someday to become a Buddhist priest himself. His father encouraged him to take up sumo wrestling and swimming to improve his weak body. His realization on the value and necessity of becoming stronger came after his father was attacked by a gang of thugs.

In Tokyo in 1901, he devoted himself to the study of jujutsu and swordsmanship. He later served with distinction during the Russo-Japanese War of 1904-1905 as a Japanese infantryman. Amazingly, he could perceive when a bullet was coming his way even before it was fired. While still fighting at the front, he worked on his physical strength and built himself to a rock-hard 170 pounds standing at five-feet, one-inch tall.

Preceding the war, Morihei moved with his family to the wilderness of Hokkaido. It was here that he attained unbelievable strength through the daily labor of working with lumber. Historically, the most significant event in his stay in Hokkaido was his meeting with Sokaku Takeda. Takeda was the grandmaster of daito-tyu aiki-jutsu and was also a master swordsman. Morihei proved no match for Sokaku. Because of his respect for Sokaku, he built a dojo in Hokkaido and invited him to live there.

He left Hokkaido when he learned that his father was gravely ill. On his way home, he stopped at the headquarters of the new Omoto-kyo religion. The Omoto-kyo religion was a mixture of Shinto mythology, shamanism and faith-healing. Morihei was deeply affected and commented that while Sokaku opened his eyes to the essence of budo, his enlightenment came through his Omoto-kyo experiences.

Morihei vividly recalls that the enlightenment took place one spring day in 1925. There was an encounter with a kendo instructor who came to test his reputation. As the instructor's wooden sword (*bokken*) cut and thrust, Morihei easily avoided the blows until his opponent stopped from exhaustion, unable to touch him. Afterward, he went out into his garden to rest. Suddenly he felt bathed in a heavenly light; the ground quaked and a golden cloud came up from earth and entered his body. It was as if the barriers between the spiritual and material worlds crumbled — "I am the universe." He was uplifted, simply delighted as tears rolled down his cheeks in an expression of gratitude to heaven and earth. It was in a flash of light that he perceived the truth and realized he became one with the universe. At that moment, he felt the true purpose of budo was love, love that cherishes and nourishes all beings. He was 42 at the time.

To quote Morihei, "The martial arts are not concerned with brute force to knock opponents down, nor with lethal weapons that lead the world into destruction. Therefore, martial training is not training that has as its primary purpose the defeating of others, but practice of God's love within ourselves." Each person is bound by his physical capabilities; but the potential for unlimited resources lies within the inner person. Morihei understood that the real battle of life is to overcome the qualities of pettiness, ambition and selfishness that keep our full potential from unfolding. He saw that budo (the way of the warrior) should follow the laws of nature, be in harmony with them and serve to protect them. The aim of the martial arts should be to achieve a state of mind united with the universe itself. His new art would become a physical reflection of spiritual beliefs. The aims of the followers of the martial arts would be to become a person in harmony with others and to become an integrated and balanced individual.

In 1927, Morihei moved to Tokyo and opened a *dojo* (practice hall). He taught there until World War II emptied his dojo of its most promising pupils. When World War II began, he left the dojo, built a hut in the mountains of Ibaragi Prefecture and engaged in farming. After that, he did not accept any new students and only allowed a few students who were deeply attached to him to train.

For some time after the war, Morihei remained in the mountains, training. He was deeply saddened by the low morale and loss of self-confidence of the Japanese that followed the war. Many people denied the existence of any spirit or God. It was at this time he called his former students together to spread the practice of aikido. The timing was right to reveal the proper use of mind and body and to let people understand the principles of Nature so that they could once again gain back their confidence.

With the rapid spread of aikido after the war, Morihei became the world-famous Professor Ueshiba or fondly called "O-Sensei" (great teacher). Up until the end of his life, he continued refining and improving his techniques — never losing his dedication to hard training. Early on the morning of April 26, 1969, Morihei took his son's hand and said, "Take care of things" and died. He was 86 years old.

Ethical Defense

Aikido is sometimes referred to as the "non-fighting art." Most experts agree that aikido is the most ethical system of martial art because of the basic principle of aiki (harmony) when dealing with an attack.

Let's explain by using the following example: A man attempts to punch an innocent passerby in the stomach. What should be the defense used by the person attacked? Should he block the strike and attempt to break the person's arm in the process? Should he then smash the attacker's face, sweep him to the ground and kick the person until he is unconscious? On one end of the spectrum some people would even justify killing this person. According to the teachings of Master Ueshiba, the person who was attacked should defend himself without hurting the other person.

Ki (or Chi)

The student in aikido is taught to respect the body of his opponent. Although many of the techniques in aikido are painful, the pain is momentary and should never create any permanent damage. Injuring your opponent is a sign of lack of control and skill and is certainly not a display of the highest level of ethics.

A man's body (arms, legs, head, joints) has obvious structural limitations as to how far it can be twisted or bent before it will break. Aikido techniques are employed to neutralize the aggressor and not harm or seriously injure him. To be able to do this requires that the aikidoist has the highest ethical intention known to man: love and respect for one another.

Ki — Universal and Individual

What is *ki*? This is one of the questions most frequently asked. In aikido the word ki is used to describe inner power or spirit; and we recognize it as our primary source of energy. Therefore, we constantly train to develop and cultivate it to the highest possible level. There are many kinds of mental power in the world that can be used to perform all sorts of tricks. These powers may be thought of as short bursts of concentrated energy. Sometimes they're useful, more often they are simply entertainment. There is only one kind of true ki, however, and it is like a vast river, never changing in volume or in the force of its flow. The whole universe is made of ki and though all people have ki, in most cases it is untapped, undeveloped and uncontrolled. Since everything has ki, no simple definition will be adequate. Some of the words that we use in our attempt to define ki are energy, intention, spirit, vital or life force.

In Oriental thought, ki is considered a submicroscopic piece of matter or energy. Something must have formed the universe. This "something" or ki is called God or Buddha, depending upon your cultural background. If we accept this reasoning, we can theorize that the heavens and earth were formed by the endless joining together of submicroscopic pieces of matter. Man, earth, and the heavens were born from ki and return to ki. The universe moves and throbs with energy; energized matter in various forms bombards earth constantly. Man takes in this energy in various ways (eating, breathing, etc.), becomes "energized" and displays various energy levels in all of his daily activities.

The mind rules and leads the body. In emergency situations, we are all capable of extraordinary mental and physical feats. All of our energy or ki is focused on the task at hand. We are completely in the "here and now." Mentally and physically we are unified to get the job done, whatever the circumstances. When someone is attacked in a self-defense situation, the mugger or rapist turns his mind to the attack before his body. This can be called the mental projection of ki. Part of the training in aikido is to feel or sense this mental force before it has been launched.

From a moral and ethical point of view, ki can be misapplied or negatively applied. There exists, therefore, strong ki, weak ki, negative and positive ki. It is believed by most masters of the martial arts that "might" (strong ki) may not be automatically "right." A strong or well-developed ki should be based upon a solid moral and ethical foundation. The indiscriminate use of force in aikido is not tolerated.

In the martial arts, when neither balance (posture) nor breathing is correct, it is impossible to have strong ki. To obtain maximum speed of technique, the muscles must be relaxed. The body, the mind, and the spirit must be balanced for efficient use or projection of ki. There is a Japanese expression, *yowaki*, that means, "this person has weak ki," and another, *tsuyoki*, meaning that "ki is strong." What differs from person to person is the way each transforms this vital energy. When ki has escaped, the Japanese use the word *gai yuku*. If a person is alive there is ki present.

If ki is both mental and physical energy, it makes sense that a person will be more efficient if the energy is centralized rather than scattered. Through practice at the dojo we must strive to feel and experience the coordination of mind and body. It is quite obvious that the entire body is stronger and can generate more power than its individual parts (arms, legs, etc.).

The Founder of aikido stated:

> I undertook the training of my body through budo, and when I realized its ultimate essence, I gained an even higher truth. I saw clearly that human beings must unify mind and body and the ki that connects the two and that a person must harmonize his activity with the activity of all things in the universe. Through the subtle working of ki, mind and body are harmonized and the relationship between the individual and the universe is harmonized.

> If the subtle working of ki is not properly utilized, a person's mind and body will become unhealthy, the world will become chaotic, and the entire universe will be thrown into disorder.

It must be emphasized that one cannot come to an understanding of ki by merely reading this book. Ki is something that must be experienced and felt through rigorous training. One will understand by staying on the path.

Misogi or Ki Breathing

Most masters of the martial arts feel that unless proper breath control is mastered, the student's progress will be limited. As stated before, the potential energy in man is usually in an uncoordinated and uncontrolled state. One method aimed at coordinating this energy is through the practice of abdominal (deep) breathing. The two most popular positions in deep breathing are *seiza* (Japanese style) or *zazen* (cross-legged). Seiza requires the student to kneel with knees approximately two fists apart and the buttocks touching the heels. In either position, the back should be straight and the rest of the body relaxed to breathe as deeply as possible. The air is drawn in slowly through the nose with the glottis at the back of the throat used to control the stream of air. As the student breathes in, the abdominal muscles should relax, allowing the central and lower part of the body (from *hara* up), not just the chest, to expand. To see how this is done, watch a baby breathe and be aware of the belly and chest going in and out.

The air fills the upper torso from the bottom to the top as though you were filling a glass. Care should be taken not to strain or tense up during any part of the breathing. At the end of the breath, one should allow the mind and the breath to settle at the one-point (hara). The mouth is used for exhalation, making the sound "aah" as the air is released. The inhalation and exhalation are both done slowly, taking approximately eight-to-ten seconds for each. This deep breathing method allows the mind and body to relax and center itself. Your mind can entertain one thought at one moment; and, therefore, if you are centered on your breathing, you cannot at the same time be thinking of something else — job, money, girlfriend, etc.

Recent medical literature states that 70-80 percent of modern diseases are caused by psychosomatic or nervous disorders. The majority of people get nervous, angry, and worry incessantly and, therefore, tense the body. A sick person breathes very shallow and fast; a healthy person breathes in long, slow breaths. By consciously concentrating on the breath, one can positively affect the spirit and welfare of the body.

Leading and Blending

When executed properly, the techniques of aikido do not result in using brute force or clashing with the power of the opponent. Aikido in many instances employs circular motion to contend with an attack coming head-on. The attack of the opponent is not stopped but is allowed to continue. The aikidoist joins with the power of the attack and then redirects this power harmlessly and harmoniously. Taking the attack and redirecting it is called "leading" the opponent's energy or intention.

Again, there should be no strain in the execution of techniques (especially in the upper body). The aikidoist will let the opponent go where he wants to go, return to where he wants to go, and bend in the direction he wants to bend. As the technique continues, the attacker is allowed to fall where he wants to fall — effortlessly and naturally.

There is a limit to what you can accomplish with brute strength. If you stand on a railroad track and try to stop the train, you will, as we say in aikido, become one with the tracks! Not a pleasant sight. It is much easier and effective to move off the track and blend with the train's power. In aikido much time is spent on getting "off the line" and not clashing or blocking as in other martial arts. It should not be a contest of power against power.

Dojo Etiquette

When entering a dojo, shoes must be removed and put in their proper place.

Dress promptly and remove all jewelry, watch, rings, necklace, etc.

Students should bow when stepping on and off the mat and should also bow to each other before and after each training session.

Students should bow to the instructor when called to assist with a technique and before returning to their sitting place.

When the instructor corrects or helps you with a technique, acknowledge with a bow and a thank you.

If a student is late, he should have the instructor's permission before he joins the class. After receiving permission, if the warm-up exercises are in progress, he should blend with what's being done at the time, and if additional warm-up time is required, he should do so on his own time. Proper warm-up is a must to help eliminate injuries.

Hygiene is not only important for your own health and well-being but consideration should be given to the people you train with, as no one in his right mind cherishes the idea of training with an unclean and smelly person.

A clean body and clean uniform are very appropriate. Finger nails and toe nails should be clean and trimmed, as jagged nails can scratch or cut someone.

To be friendly, courteous and grateful for the knowledge you are receiving is the best dojo etiquette that I know of.

Attitude

One of the first things you notice about a person is his attitude. Your attitude toward life and others is one of the most powerful generating forces on earth. If your attitude and thoughts are positive, your life will reflect positive results. Our jails are filled with people who have negative attitudes toward society and show no respect toward their fellow man or property. It is simple to understand that a criminal first performs the crime in his mind.

When you see a person who has a proper attitude it tells you that his energy is positive. Positive attitude produces enthusiasm which in turn generates energy. Positive-thinking people accomplish more life goals because they expect positive results. Belief creates the actual fact! You create your own reality. Take a situation where you're asked to do a certain job at work. Do the job without complaints and do it with pride. Whether it's a small or big job is not important; what's important is that you put your heart into it. This means doing your very best.

Another way in which attitude plays a big part in your life is how you handle problems. Everyone has problems. With a good attitude problems become challenges. Learn to expect problems and use them to make you a stronger person. If you do experience a failure or setback, say to yourself — "That's not like me, I'll do better next time." It's never too late to change your attitude. It's only when you give up and stop caring that you commit mental and physical suicide. You become your own worst enemy. You lose the harmonious balance of mind and body.

One way you can change your attitude, too, is to adopt the spirit of thankfulness. Most people go around in life only aware of what they want or don't have. Concentrate on your strengths. Be thankful for your food, clothing, shelter and for people who appreciate and love you.

Treasure your time. Most people live their lives as if they had all the time in the world. Think about how much time is wasted on projects which are not of value to you or society. You must realize that what you do affects the universe as a whole. Have your life make a real difference; make it count! Learn as much as you can. This enthusiasm for learning is one of the true realities of life. It was Ralph Waldo Emerson who said, "Nothing great was ever achieved without enthusiasm."

Begin and end your day by being grateful for another chance and for the opportunities you were given to learn. Think of each day as if it were your last. Remind yourself of this constantly, and you will realize that some things are not so important anymore.

Commitment

Before embarking on the practice of aikido, you should be committed to practicing at least three days per week. A person cannot properly learn the art without consistent and diligent practice. Aikido is not merely an intellectual undertaking. You must put your body on the mat, learn through sweat and hard training. It will not be easy. There will be times when you will not want to practice — many excuses will come up for you. You must be able to stand behind your commitment. Be able to say "no thanks" to your friends when they go partying.

As a responsible student, you should inquire as to what needs to be done to maintain the upkeep of the dojo. This is part of your training. Proper courtesy should be given to welcome guests and new beginning students. Answer their questions with a helpful attitude.

There are many styles of aikido practiced in the world today. It is highly recommended that before signing up for study, you should go and watch several practices to see if that particular school is right for you. Observe the students and instructors and make an honest decision on whether you can fit in.

Exercises

The body must be stretched in every possible direction to acquire flexibility, thus making movement easier and lessening the chance of injury. In the beginning, some of these exercises and postures will be difficult and will not feel natural, but with practice and determination the desired mobility and suppleness will be achieved. In these exercises, you must aim for steady and relaxed progress. Exercises should not be seen as a purely physical activity. To gain the most from them, you must also work on concentration and breathing. Concentration and relaxation are necessary components of good training. Deep muscle relaxation is extremely important; there, you must learn to be natural and efficient. When stretching one body part you must be sure not to tense the rest of the body. Exhaling as you stretch will help relax the body and give you a better stretch.

Keeping fit should be a never-ending process. Physical fitness is not something that can be stored in the body. One must remain in a regular (at least three times per week) exercise program to maintain health. When you are doing stretching exercises, you should concentrate and focus the mind totally on each particular part of the body that is being stretched. Remember that concentrating on whatever it is that you're doing takes no more energy than daydreaming and produces better results.

There are many postures to be mastered, and it may take years of practice to become relaxed during the stretch. You can maintain suppleness into an advanced age with regular workouts. This becomes a positive way of living. Just as you practice an old negative habit, you can learn to substitute a positive one in its place. The amount of work is the same. Sometimes you don't realize how hard you work at something that's entirely wrong for you. There's work involved in any direction you go.

Stretching

Flexibility is an often overlooked component of physical fitness. Most people become concerned about being flexible only after the joints stiffen and muscles shorten from disease, injury or just plain disuse. You must have a reasonable amount of flexibility to perform aikido and to perform efficiently in daily life. Adequate flexibility permits freedom of movement, contributes to ease and economy of muscular effort and makes you less susceptible to some types of muscular injuries.

There are two basic types of stretching exercises — static (passive) and ballistic (bouncing). To develop flexibility, the muscles must be stretched longer than its normal length. Whether you are doing static or ballistic stretch, the muscle must be stretched about ten percent beyond its normal length. When stretching, minimal pain may result, but excessive pain is not desirable and should be understood as the body telling you that you are exceeding your limits.

Static stretching exercises involve a slow sustained stretching of a muscle. When executing this type of stretch, you slowly lengthen the muscle and hold it in the lengthened position for at least ten-to-fifteen seconds. In the stretched position you should breathe slowly and evenly, trying to relax as much as possible. Because static stretching is safer (less chance to overstretch the muscle), it is recommended that you precede ballistic stretching with a slow holding stretch during your workouts.

Ballistic stretching involves bouncing or jerking so the momentum of a body part will help you increase the stretch placed on a muscle. As stated before, exhale when stretching the muscle or group of muscles and inhale as your body comes back to the original position.

Kiatsu — Pressing with Ki

In many aikido dojo, *kiatsu* (a form of acupressure) is practiced as part of the workout. When one has energy locked in an area of the body, pressure is administered to help free that energy so that it can flow back into the meridians of the body. Kiatsu is not a cure, however, but a type of preventive care.

Kiatsu is like recharging a drained battery. It is important, however, to note that the person giving the kiatsu treatment should also receive it back, so that he is not left drained of his energy. That is aiki.

Kiatsu can be administered to someone when he is seated or lying down. Most of the time kiatsu is done along the side of the spinal column. The thumbs are used for the pressure and are angled slightly in. The person who is giving kiatsu should press with his one-point (body weight) so that his hands won't tire. As you press in with the thumbs, both people should exhale. After you have pressed, inhale and move your thumbs approximately one inch and repeat the procedure.

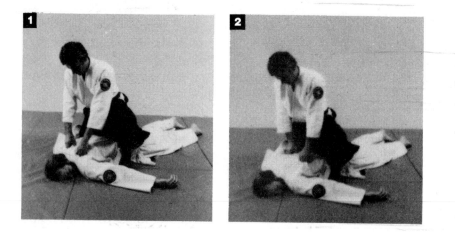

HOW TO FOLD A HAKAMA

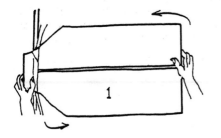

1

6

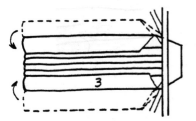

2

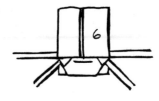

7

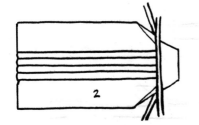

3

8

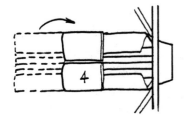

4

9

10   11

5

12   13   14

Extension of Ki

Picture 1 is an example of improper extension of ki or awareness. Statistics show that you are more likely to be attacked with this type of body language. Picture 2 is an example of extending ki properly with good posture. It is obvious that in this picture you can see and react to danger more efficiently.

Seiza — Proper Way of Sitting. Photograph 1 shows proper posture while seated. The back should be straight with the shoulders relaxed. The back of the neck is stretched up with the chin slightly tucked. The knees are placed approximately two or three fists apart. The feet are tucked under with the left big toe crossing over the right toe. The buttocks should be touching the heels. Weight is underside. Picture 2 is an example of improper posture. In this position you are unable to breathe deeply and are more easily thrown or knocked off balance. If you cannot display proper posture sitting, you undoubtedly will have problems standing and moving efficiently.

Bowing. When training in aikido, we bow to each other to show respect and appreciation. Bowing is the way you show your gratitude to your teacher and to your partner while practicing. From seiza, the left hand is placed on the mat followed by the right hand. The hands form a triangle and the body is lowered. You then return to seiza.

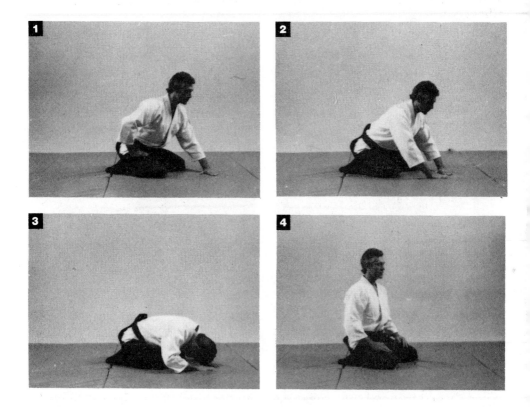

Stances

Hanmi. Proper footwork is essential to the execution of aikido. The basic stance in aikido is called *hanmi*. Your body weight should be evenly distributed with the feet approximately one shoulder width apart. The back foot is turned out and the front foot is pointed at a 45-degree angle. Pictures 1 and 2 show proper hanmi with either right or left leg forward.

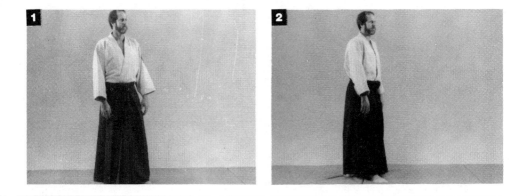

Maai. When practicing with a partner, proper distance between the two people is necessary for correct execution of technique. Distance should be controlled by the nage. A common method to check for proper maai is to assume a hanmi stance while extending the front arm. The fingertips of the uke and nage should touch.

Ai-hanmi and Gyaku-hanmi. As the uke prepares to attack, the nage will either be in *ai-hanmi* (mutual stance) or *gyaku-hanmi* (opposite stance). In ai-hanmi both people will have the same foot forward. Picture 1 shows ai-hanmi with uke and nage both having their left foot forward. Picture 2 is an example of gyaku-hanmi. In this picture, the uke has his right foot forward and the nage has his left foot in front. As you study the techniques in this book, pay special attention to the stances and footwork. Proper stance and balance are the foundation for strong, well-executed techniques.

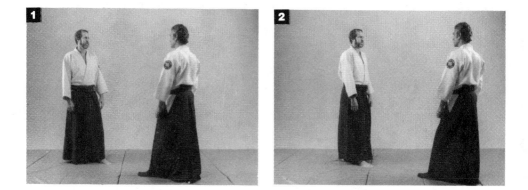

Uniform. The uniform worn in aikido is called a *gi*. In most aikido schools the student wears a colored belt to signify his rank in class. After obtaining the rank of brown or black belt (shodan), the student is allowed to wear a hakama (a long pants-skirt formal wear).

Stretching Exercises

Neck Circles. Rotate the neck in a full range of motion (in every direction).

Shoulder Rotations. Circle the arms forward and backward.

Shoulder Stretch. Interlock your fingers behind your neck and bend forward at the waist. This exercise stretches the shoulders, lower back and the back of the legs (hamstrings). Be sure to keep your elbows and knees straight to get the most out of the stretch.

Trunk Rotation. While maintaining your balance, rotate your upper body in a clockwise direction and then in a counterclockwise direction. Rotate in each direction at least five times.

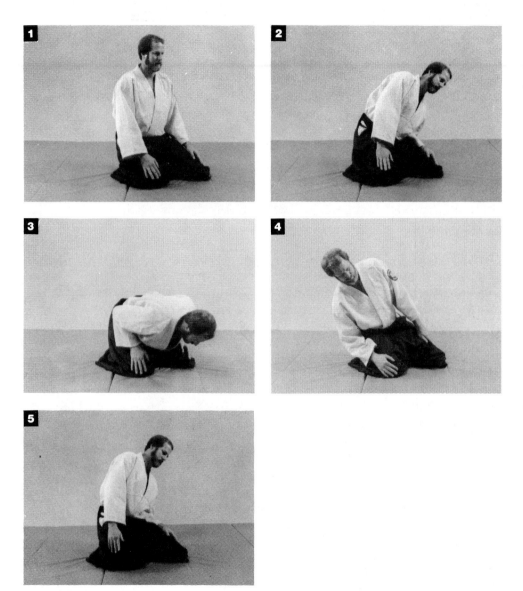

Back Stretch. From seiza, spread your heels apart (about one foot) and lean back as far as you can comfortably go. When you first begin to try this exercise, use your hands or elbows to support your body weight. This exercise stretches the lower back and the top of the thighs.

Forward Stretch. With your legs together, stretch forward as far as possible. You should pull your toes back and keep the knees straight to get the maximum stretch. This stretch can be performed by holding the position as shown or by sitting up and bouncing forward. You should feel the stretch in your lower back and the back of your legs.

Spread Leg Stretch. To begin the stretch, spread the legs as wide as possible. From this position bring the head and chest down to the knee. Try to keep the back as flat as possible. In the second exercise, the ear is brought down to the knee and the head should be between the arm and the leg. This stretches the waist and rib cage. The next picture shows a forward action with the legs even wider than before. Bring the chest and head down as far as possible. Remember to keep the back flat.

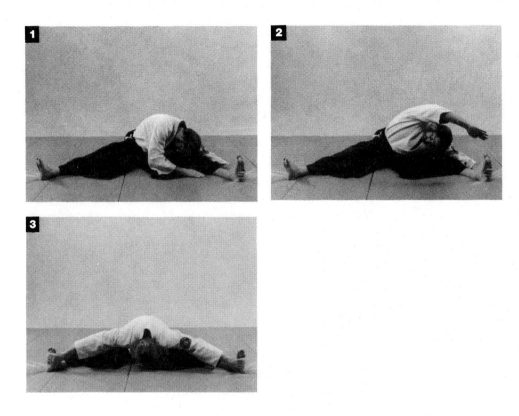

Butterfly Stretch. Bring the soles of your feet together and pull your heels as close to your groin as possible. Bounce the knees up and down — rapid movement. To stretch the lower back and hips, pull the chin down to the toes. Repeat at least five times.

Hip Stretch. While holding the feet, place one hand on your knee and gently push down. Raise the knee up and push down again. Repeat at least five times on each side.

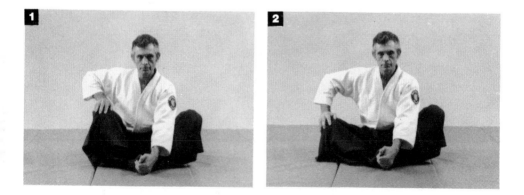

Leg Cross Over. This exercise is intended to stretch the muscles of the hip and lower back. With your hands 90 degrees from the body (palms down), lift one leg up as high as possible. Roll the leg across your body and then look in the opposite direction. The next set of pictures shows a similar stretch done on your stomach. With your chin on the ground, lift one leg as high as possible. Hold the leg approximately five seconds and then cross the leg over. This exercise strengthens the lower back and also stretches that area.

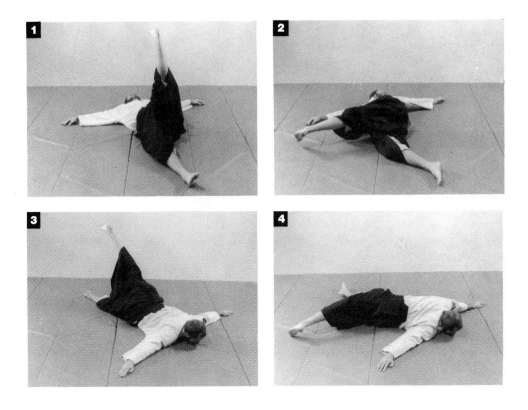

Cobra. Place your hands under your shoulders and push up as high as you can comfortably go, leading with the chin. Keep the hips on the mat and arch the lower back. Come down slowly and relax completely for about ten seconds. Repeat.

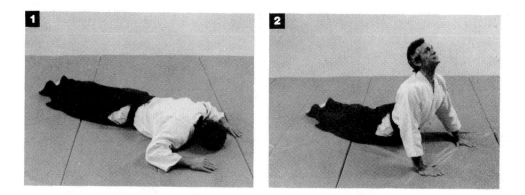

Mini-Split. From seiza, spread the knees as wide as possible. Let the weight of your hips drop down and relax. You can also push your hips back toward your heels. Rock front to back to obtain a better stretch.

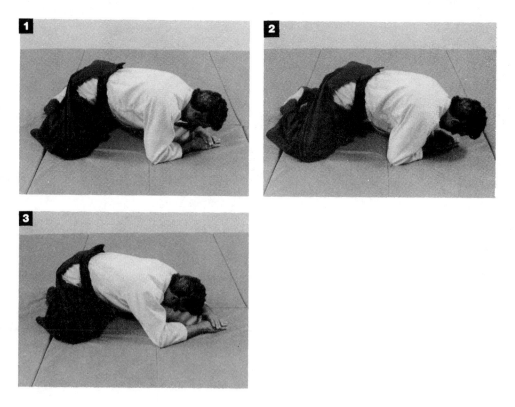

Outer Hip Stretch. The following stretch loosens the outside of the hip and is excellent preparation for flexibility used in tumbling. Take your right leg and extend it 90 degrees to the left. The left leg is extended straight back. Let your hips drop straight down and relax. Gently rock back and forth.

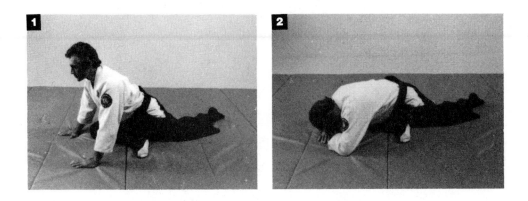

Hamstring Stretch — Leg isolation. From a right hanmi stance bend forward as far as possible. Keep the left leg bent and straighten the front leg with the toes pulled back. Hold the stretch on each side for approximately ten seconds.

Knee Rotation. Bend the knees slightly and rotate in a complete circle. (Do several times in each direction).

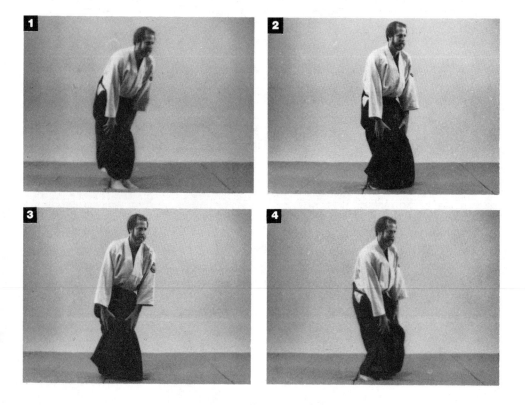

Stomach Exercises

Crunches. Knees should be bent with feet flat on the ground. Clasp your hands behind your head. Bring your shoulders and head forward. Try to put your chin on your navel.

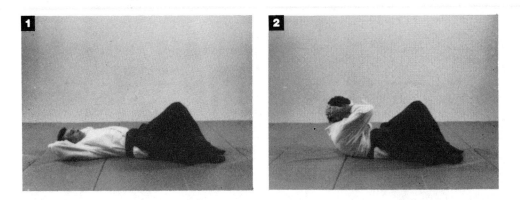

Cross Overs. From the same starting position as the crunches, sit up and bring your right elbow to your left knee and your left elbow to your right knee.

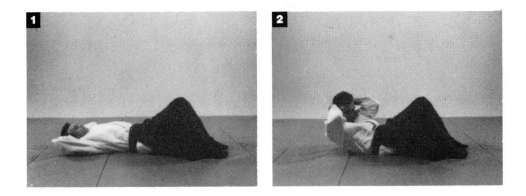

Leg Toss. One person assumes a standing position with his feet straddling his partner's head. The person lying down grabs the ankles of the person standing. Keeping the knees straight, lift the feet up to your partner's chest. The person standing grabs the ankles and pushes them toward the ground. You should stop your feet as close to the ground as possible without letting them touch. Repeat 10-to-20 times.

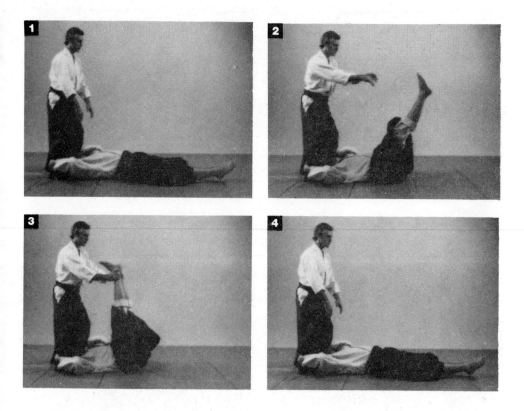

Wrist Exercises

It is important to warm up and strengthen the wrists as well as the rest of the body before performing *waza* (techniques) in aikido practice. Many aikido techniques involve twisting the wrists in various directions, causing momentary pain to the uke. It is therefore important for the aikidoist to have strong flexible wrists. The shoulders should be relaxed and down and you should extend ki out both hands during the exercises.

Kotegaeshi Undo. The exercise starts by grasping the hand with the thumb between the last two knuckles, and the bottom three fingers grabbing the base of the thumb. Pictures 3 and 4 show the outward and downward direction of the wrist bend or turn out. The wrist is pulled down to the one-point.

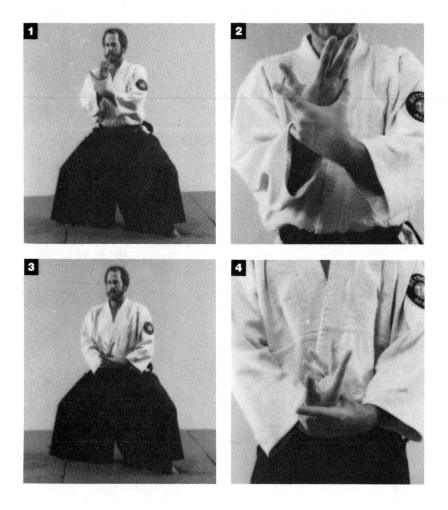

Nikkyo Undo. Place your left palm over the back of the right hand. Apply force to the first two knuckles. Be sure to extend ki with both hands while performing the exercise.

Sankyo Undo. Grab the blade of your right hand with the left. Point the fingers of the right hand down as you crank the hand out to the side of your body. Keep your right arm perpendicular to the ground.

Tekubi Shindo Undo — Wrist shaking exercise. Relax and shake your wrists as fast as possible. Imagine that you are spraying the ground with ki. Move from your one-point. The entire body should shake if you are properly relaxed.

Funakogi Undo — Rowing exercise. The purpose of this exercise is to learn to move properly from your one-point when grabbed by the wrists. The exercise starts with most of the weight on the front leg. The front leg is bent and the back leg straight. Movement begins with the hips moving forward first and then followed by the wrists extending. In this position the front leg is bent and the back leg should be straight. To move back, the hips again initiate the movement followed by the hands dropping back to the hips. This exercise can be performed with a partner holding your wrists so that you can test proper body movement.

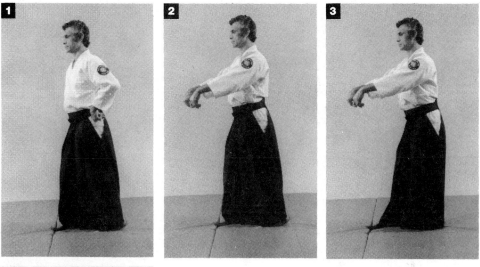

Shomenuchi Ikkyo Undo. This exercise is used to defend against a strike coming down at your forehead. Stand in right hanmi with most of your weight on the front leg. Initiate the movement with the hips followed by both arms swinging upward from the fingertips. Do not overextend your arms. The next movement is to drop your hands to your sides, followed by the hips. Let your fingers naturally curl as the hands drop.

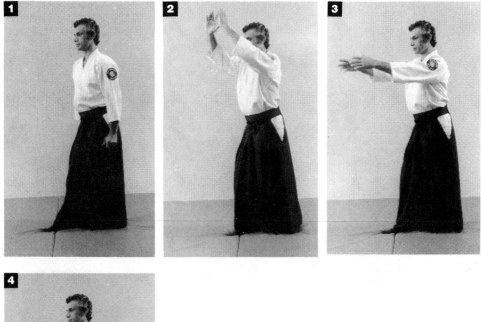

Zengo Undo — Two-directional exercise. This is the same exercise as shomenuchi ikkyo undo with a 180-degree turn. After dropping your arms, do not reverse your hips. Shift your weight to the balls of your feet and pivot. The purpose of the exercise is to learn to extend your energy in two different directions — an attack from the front and behind.

Tenkan Undo. This exercise is used to teach proper turning mechanics. From left hanmi extend your left wrist with the fingers pointed back toward your body. Slide forward with the left foot and pivot — bringing the right leg around and behind the left foot. As you complete the turn, extend your hand forward (palm facing up). You are actually turning your body around your hand. To complete the exercise, drop your left hand and extend your right wrist. Step forward with your right foot and pivot. Be sure to turn your mind completely in each direction. The mind leads the body.

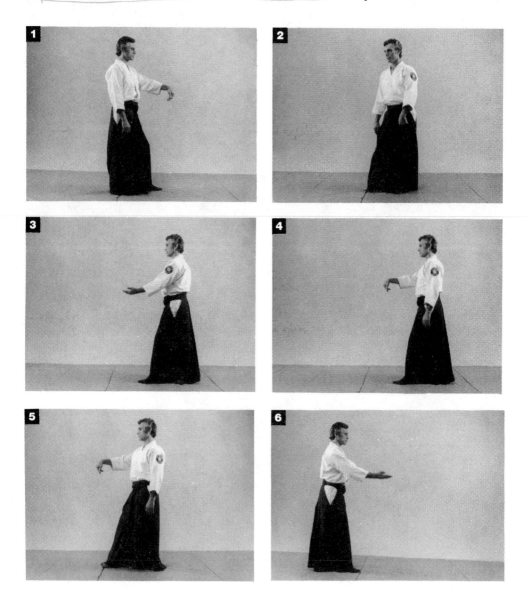

Udefuri Undo. This exercise teaches you how to extend ki out of the fingertips as the arms swing from side to side. Start with your arms on the left side. Let your arms float up and away from your body. Drop your arms down to the right hip. The weight of the arms is down (underside). This exercise promotes a loose relaxed feeling in the upper body.

Udefuri Choyaku Undo. This exercise is the same as udefuri with a 180-degree turn added. Start with your right foot forward and your hands on the left side. Slide forward with your right foot. Pivot on your right foot as you come around with the left foot, turning to your right. As you turn, the turning of your body will cause the arms to float up and out from your center. To complete the turn, step around the left foot with the right and then draw in the left leg. The arms drop and curl around to the right.

Ushiro Tekubi-Tori Zenshin Undo — Forward extension. Bend your wrist slightly and extend your fingertips forward. As your hands move forward and up, the wrists will turn over and the fingers point down. While your hands are moving up, step forward and lower yourself with a bow. The purpose of this exercise is to control a wrist-grab from behind.

Ushiro Tekubi-Tori Kotai Undo — Backstepping. This exercise teaches you proper body movement when the wrists are grabbed from behind. In this aikitaiso you will end up to the side and slightly behind the uke. You will step back at an angle as the fingers extend upward. As the hands reach chest level, the wrists turn over and the fingers point down. Step back with the opposite leg and take a bow. Extend ki out your wrists.

Sayu Undo — Lateral swing. Feet should be about shoulder width apart. The left arm is extended and unbendable with the right hand at your one-point with weight underside. Arms swing to the right as the right knee bends and the left leg straightens. Repeat the swing and extension to the left side. The uke receives a "clothesline" effect.

Sayu Undo — Backstep. This exercise is done like the previous aikitaiso with an added backstep (stepping behind) and looking in the direction of the arm swing.

Ushiro Tori Zenpo Nage. Bend your elbows and point your fingers forward with the palms up as you step forward. The forward foot should end up in line or directly in front of the back foot so that the attacker is thrown around the body instead of over the hips. As the arms continue to extend forward, the hands will rotate palms down. As the front foot plants, the hips are twisted and your ki is extended forward.

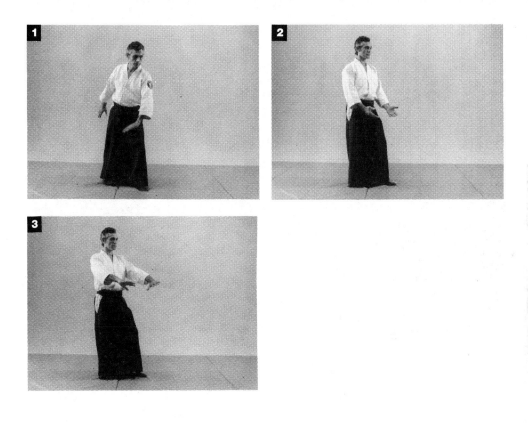

Koho Tento Undo — Backward roll. This exercise is the basis or foundation for learning to tumble forward and backward. The starting position is with the back straight and eyes extended forward. The shoulders are relaxed. As you roll backward, you will roll to one side of your spine with your attention forward. The chin is tucked in so that the head does not touch the floor or mat. Rock forward to the starting position. The bottom leg should be flat on the mat from the knee to the ankle. The front foot should be in line with the center of your body or approximately a foot in front of the bottom leg.

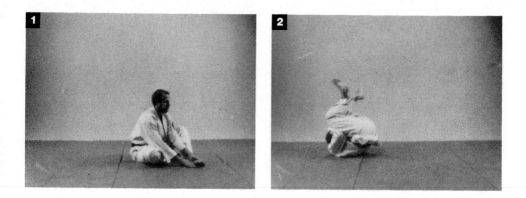

Tekubi Kosa Undo — Double wrist break. In this exercise the wrists are crossed in front of your one-point. You should alternate crossing the wrists. The purpose of this exercise is to move your hands efficiently when grabbed by both wrists.

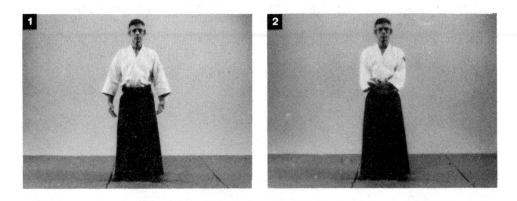

Tekubi Joho Kosa Undo — High wrist break. Swing the arms up and cross your wrists about neck level. Arms should be unbendable.

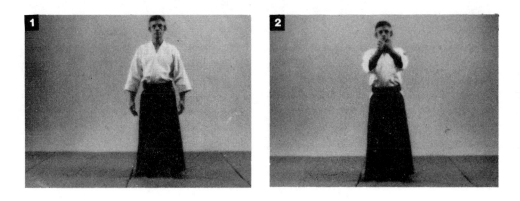

Ukemi — Tumbling. From a kneeling position with the right foot forward, drop down to the bottom part of the left leg and begin to make your body round. Extend your right arm approximately 30 degrees from your body. Reach across with the left arm and touch the mat behind your right shoulder. Be sure to keep the right arm extended. Draw your knees over the right shoulder and assume an upright and stable posture. Extend ki forward.

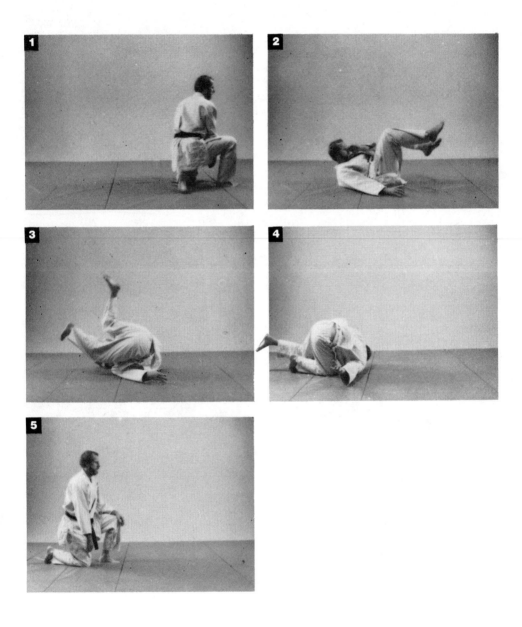

Standing — Roll backward and stand up. From a standing position drop down on the back leg and roll backward with chin tucked in. Stand up with good posture. Keep arms down and shoulders relaxed.

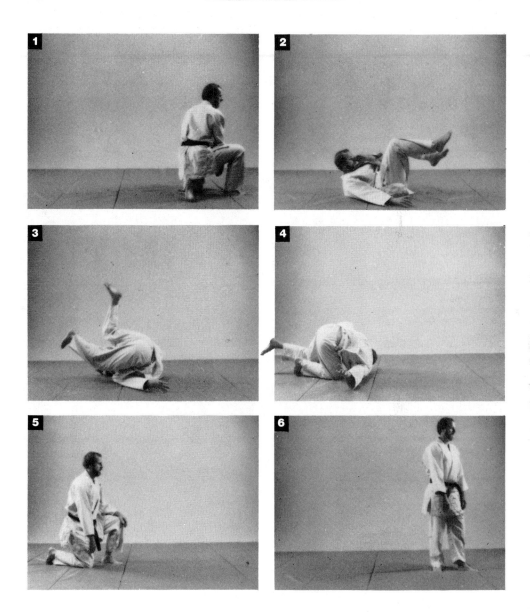

Forward — From knees. Starting from a kneeling position, lean forward and place the blade of the forward hand on the mat with the little finger touching first. The arm should be kept unbendable throughout the roll so that you do not take the impact of the roll on the elbow or shoulder. Although you are rolling over the shoulder, the direction of the tumble should be straight ahead. As you roll onto your back, keep your body round and continue the tumble until your center of gravity (one-point) has moved over the bottom leg.

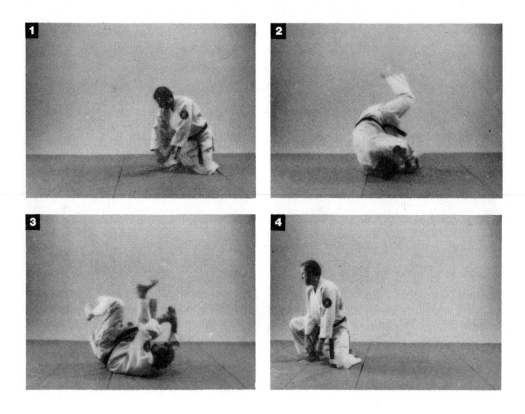

Standing — Forward. Begin in a standing position with the feet approximately shoulder width apart (hanmi). Point the fingers back toward the body to avoid injury to the wrist. Keep the arm unbendable and tumble over your shoulder. Your head should not touch the mat. Roll over the bottom leg and stand up with good posture.

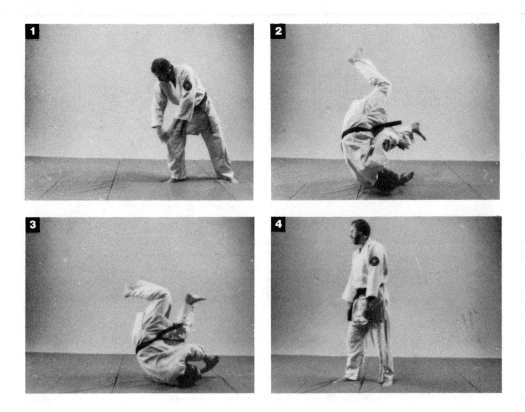

Leaping — Forward. After you are proficient with the standing tumble, you are ready to learn the tumble with a forward leap — covering height and distance. Push off the supporting leg while extending the forward arm. Again the arm should be unbendable with the fingers pointing back. Roll up the side of the arm and over the shoulder. Make your body as round as possible.

Push From Front — Backward tumble. Tumbling is the same standing backward roll as shown earlier. Have your partner push you down and back to create a "streetlike" situation. Be sure to keep the chin tucked.

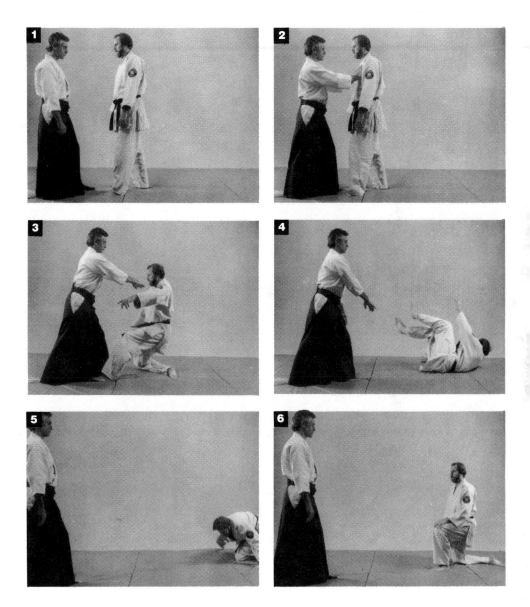

Push From Back — Forward tumble. Have your partner push you forward and down. Be sure you have learned the forward roll adequately before attempting this with a partner.

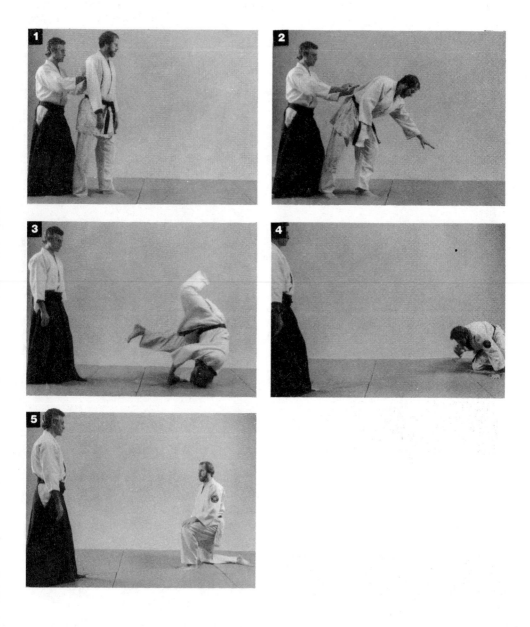

Samurai Walk. The purpose of the samurai walk is to strengthen the lower body and learn to move efficiently from the one-point. Many of the techniques that are practiced standing can be done also from the kneeling position (*suwari waza*). When you move forward, take a step, placing your entire foot in contact with the mat. Swing one knee forward until the knee points straight ahead and the foot is flat underneath the knee. As you bring the knee forward and down, the heels come together forming a right angle.

Atemi — Proper attacks. It is extremely important that you learn to attack properly. All attacks should be sincere and should be delivered with proper focus. It is impossible to practice correctly without realistic attacks from the uke.

Shomenuchi — Strike to nage's forehead. Starting position for uke is with the feet one-to-one-and-a-half shoulder width apart. As you step forward with the back foot, raise the hand to the center of your body with the blade of the hand facing forward. Visualize that the blade of the hand is a sword (bokken). Bring the hand down and strike directly at the nage's forehead. If the nage does not move, the blow should land in the middle of the forehead.

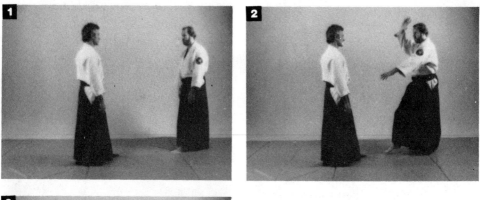

Munetsuki — Punch to midsection. From a hanmi stance, step forward with the back leg. The punch is delivered from the rear hip and comes in a straight line from the hip toward the center of the nage's stomach. Do not hook the punch.

Yokomenuchi — Side strike. As you step forward, raise the hand in front of the body. The strike then starts to go out in a circle and comes around to the side of nage's head. The strike can be with the blade of the hand or with the fist (hook punch).

Kata Tori — Shoulder grab. Step forward and reach directly toward nage's shoulder. As in all attacks, the uke should sincerely try to grab the nage's shoulder. The attack should be smooth and continuous.

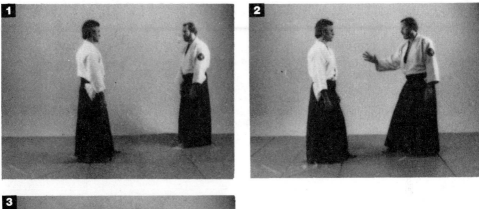

Extension of Ki

Unbendable arm. Unbendable arm is an exercise in which you can feel the difference between proper ki or energy extension and brute strength. The first attempt is made by tensing the arm as much as possible, and making a tight fist. Uke tries to slowly bend the arm by placing one hand on the wrist and the other hand slightly above the elbow. Nage's arm may or may not bend. In the second attempt, the nage relaxes as much as possible and opens the hand and mentally extends energy through the arm and out the fingertips. Imagine that your arm is a firehose with water pouring out. The arm should feel relaxed, but not limp. Uke should apply the same amount of force as in the first attempt. The importance of this exercise is to feel the difference in the amount of energy expended in each attempt. With practice you are able to hold the arm with much less tension and can move freely rather than feeling locked in.

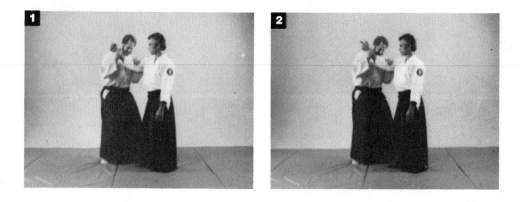

Kokyu Dosa — Sitting extension. To begin this exercise, nage extends his arms to uke. Uke holds nage's wrists. Nage extends forward from the one-point until uke's balance is disrupted. Nage then leads uke to one side (proper throwing angle). The pin is performed by placing the knife edges of your hand on the shoulder and wrist of the uke and extending downward.

Extension Ki Through Jo — Grabbing jo. Nage and uke each grab ends of the jo. Picture 1 shows nage trying to pull or move uke by using his upper body (arms and shoulders). In the next picture, nage relaxes the upper body and moves from the hips. Uke holds on until he loses his balance and takes a forward tumble. The same principle can be used when pushing with the jo. Relax, move from your hips and extend your mind through the tip of the jo. Next, nage and uke place the jo at their one-points. Nage moves from his hips and causes the uke to lose his balance.

CHAPTER 4
TECHNIQUES — WAZA

Shomenuchi Ikkyo. Starting in gyaku-hanmi, uke steps forward and strikes shomen to nage. Nage slides in before the strike starts down and applies ikkyo. Nage has his right hand at uke's wrist and his left hand on uke's elbow. As nage slides forward, he pushes uke's elbow toward his face. In this position uke's balance is broken. Nage then steps through with his left leg and immediately extends down. Nage should place his one-point above uke's elbow. As nage continues forward, uke will not be able to stand up.

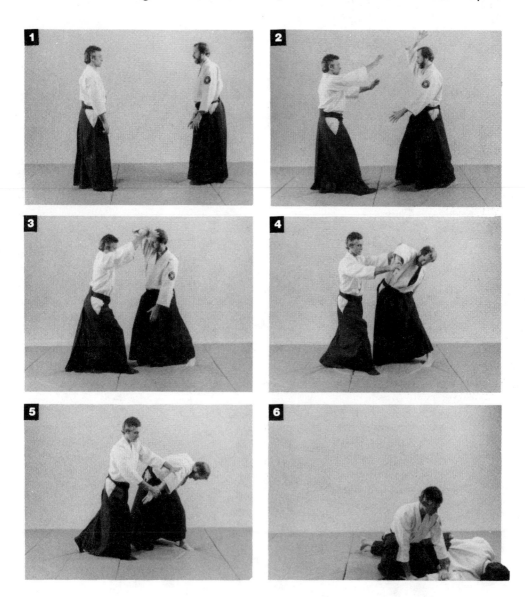

Shomenuchi Kokyunage. Uke again strikes shomen. Nage slides in and uses a tenkan movement to blend with the attack. Nage allows the strike to continue and then drops his right forearm over uke's elbow. At the same time nage's left arm goes over uke's shoulder and applies weight underside. At this point uke's balance is poor. Nage reverses his direction and brings his right arm in front of uke's face and down over his left shoulder.

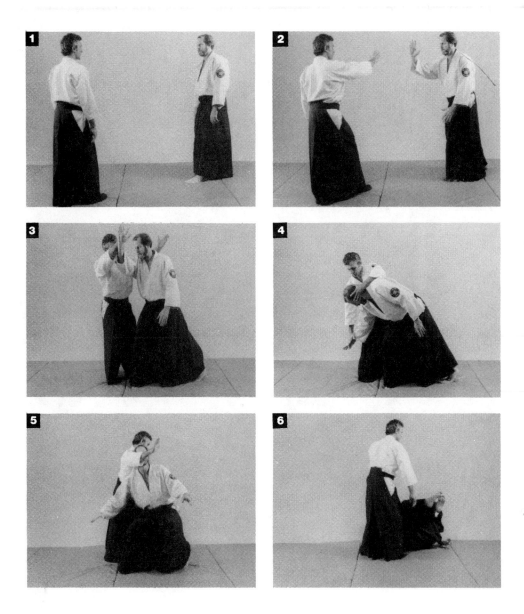

Shomenuchi Kotegaeshi. From gyaku-hanmi, nage blends with uke's shomen attack by using a tenkan movement. As the strike comes down, nage drops his hands down on uke's forearm. Nage then slides his right hand down to the uke's wrist. Nage steps to the side and back and applies kotegaeshi. To finish the technique nage rolls the uke over on his stomach. The nage walks around the uke and cranks the arm in a counterclockwise direction. He then straightens the uke's arm and places his right leg up against uke's left arm. He then pushes down on the first two knuckles of uke's hand.

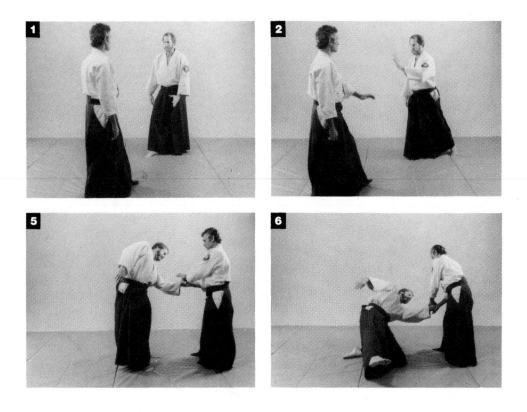

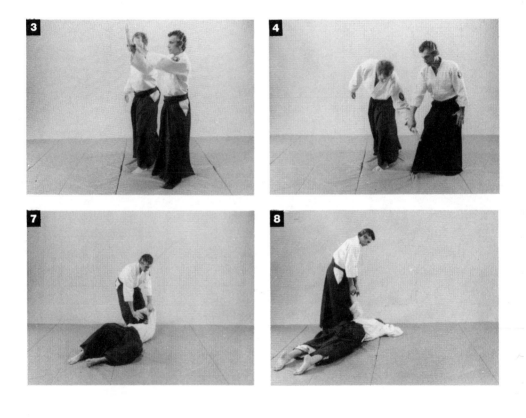

Shomenuchi Ikkyo With Tanto (Knife). Technique is the same as shomenu-chi ikkyo except the opponent has a knife. After nage takes uke down, he will take the knife away. Bend the elbow and slide uke's wrist under his elbow. Then push down on the elbow to cause pain in the wrist.

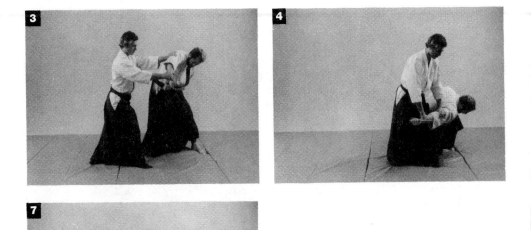

Yokomen — Side Strike

Yokomenuchi Kokyunage — Tenkan. As uke strikes yokomen, nage slides forward and uses a tenkan motion to blend with the strike. Nage applies weight underside (down) on uke's elbow and continues turning. The same technique is used against a hook punch.

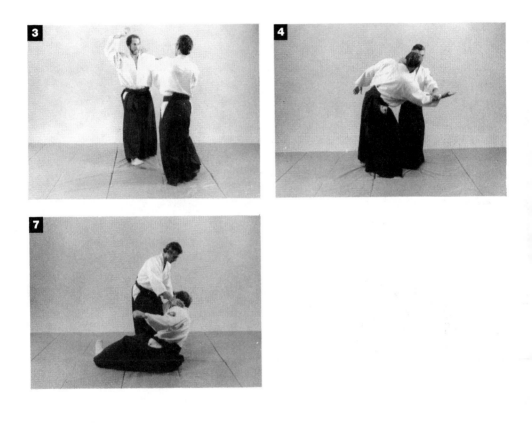

Yokomenuchi Kokyunage — Irimi. Irimi means entering. Instead of turning, nage moves into uke and applies weight underside with his left hand. The nage's right hand can either push on the chest, under the chin, or could be a strike (atemi) to the face.

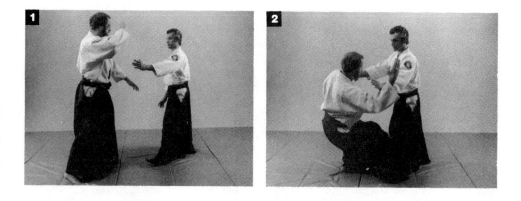

Yokomenuchi Zenponage. As yokomen comes toward nage, he misdirects the strike down and across his body. From this point, nage torques uke's hand palm up, and steps in with his left leg. Note the extension of nage's left arm. The forward movement of nage's body causes uke to fall forward.

Yokomenuchi Kokyunage — Neck throw. As uke strikes yokomen, nage steps forward and parries the blow to the outside. Simultaneously, nage performs atemi (punch) to the uke's midsection. As the uke bends forward from the atemi, nage turns in place and grabs uke's neck with the same arm that delivered the strike. Nage drops straight down and twists his upper body toward the outside knee. (The inside knee is on the mat.) If you are working with a uke who cannot breakfall, release the neck early and let him perform a forward tumble.

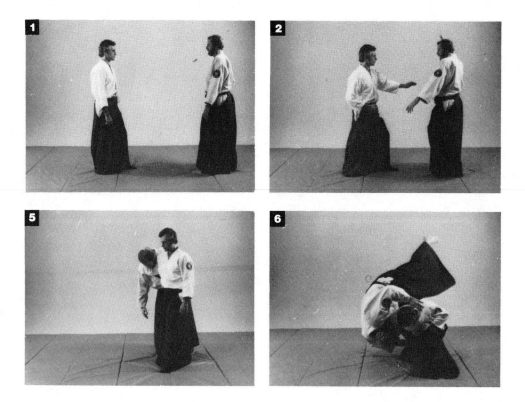

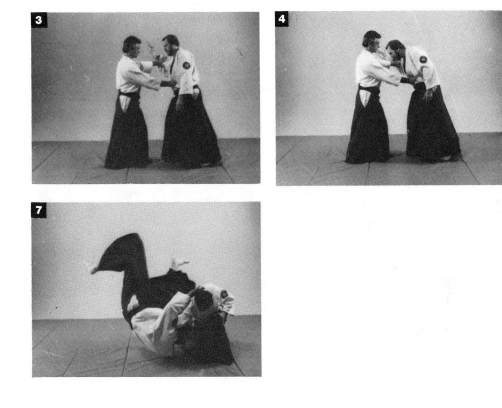

Munetsuki — Straight Punch

Munetsuki Hiji-Otoshi. Uke steps in and attempts munetsuki to nage. Nage steps to the outside and cups his hand around the uke's elbow. The nage's back hand (hand closest to uke) should be on the bottom and the front hand on top. Drop straight down on the elbow.

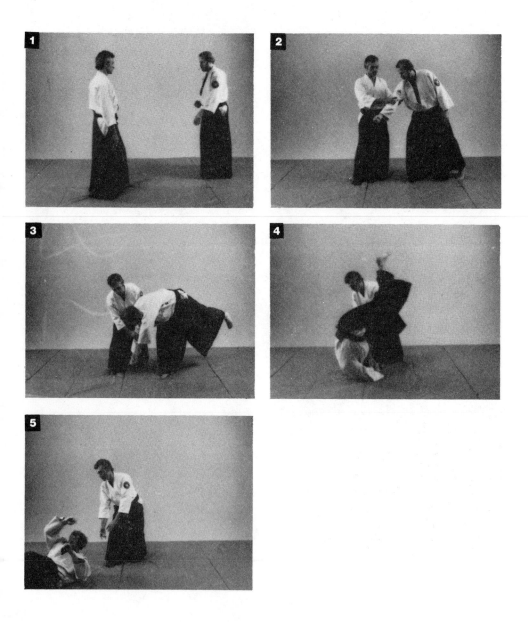

Munetsuki Zenponage. Step to the ouside and misdirect the strike across your body. Trap uke's wrist with your outside hand and extend your inside arm under uke's punch. Nage steps forward and throws uke. The proper throwing angle is the point between uke's feet which would form a triangle with the feet being the base.

Munetsuki Kotegaeshi. As uke steps in with a munetsuki attack, move to the outside and apply weight underside on the forearm of the uke. Do not attempt to grab the punch. Let your hand slide down to uke's wrist. Take a back step with the inside leg and immediately apply kotegaeshi so that the attacker cannot punch you with the free hand. To finish the technique, place one hand on the elbow and crank or turn the uke's arm in a circular direction as you walk around his head. Whenever possible, it is best to finish a technique with the uke on his stomach so that he cannot punch or kick.

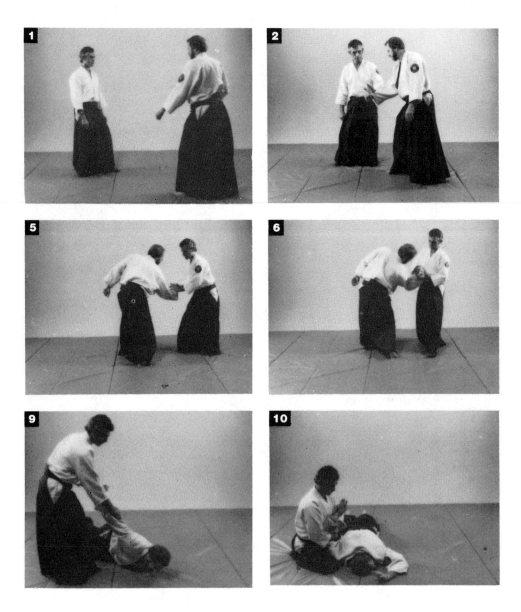

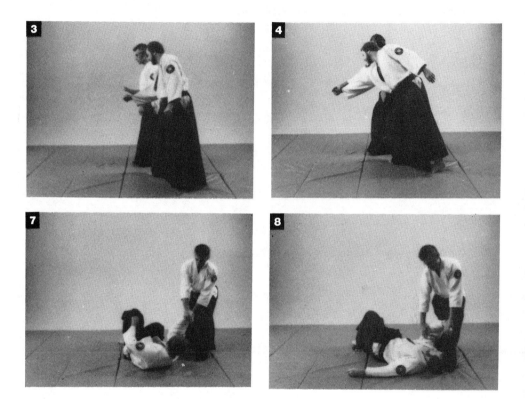

Munetsuki Kaiten-Nage. Uke steps forward and punches at nage's stomach. Nage slides off the line of attack and extends down on uke's wrist. Nage continues this circular movement with his left hand and pushes down on the back of uke's neck. To complete the throw, nage pushes uke's top arm over his head.

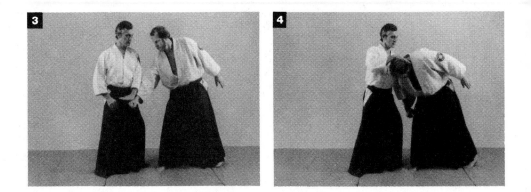

Kata Tori — Shoulder Grab

Kata Tori Ikkyo. Uke attempts to grab nage's right lapel (shoulder) with his left hand. Nage steps back with his right foot and applies weight underside with his left hand. From this position, nage makes a large circle with his left hand which is holding uke's wrist. He slides forward with the left foot and pushes uke's elbow toward his face with his right hand. He steps through with the right leg and extends down. Nage pins the uke by pushing down on the elbow and forcing the wrist to bend toward uke's forearm.

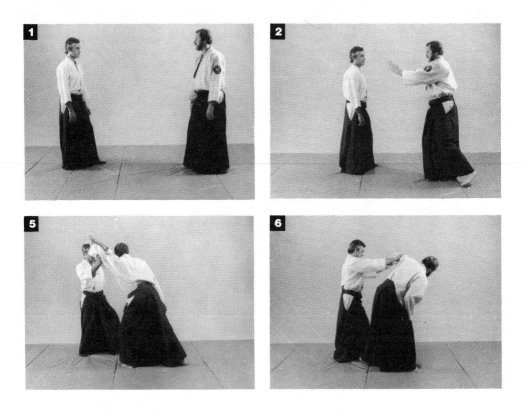

Kata Tori Nikkyo. The first part of this technique is the same as the previous ikkyo. As nage steps forward, he brings uke's wrist into his chest with the uke's fingers pointed toward nage's shoulder (thumb is down). Nage then brings his right hand over uke's arm as he draws his right hand in toward uke's wrist. (This motion is similar to scooping water.) Nage bows slightly forward. This technique can be extremely painful and should be practiced with a good deal of sensitivity. The pin is the same as above.

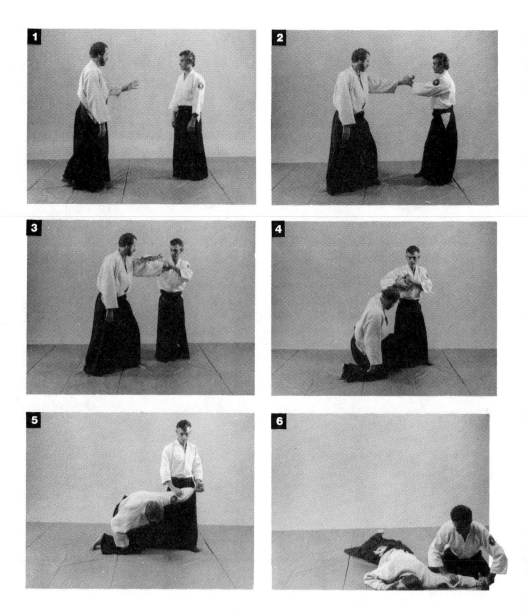

Kata Tori Sankyo. As uke attacks, nage repeats the same sequence as was shown for ikkyo. After nage performs ikkyo, he leans into uke's shoulder and extends down so that uke cannot escape. Notice the position of uke's arm under nage's body. Nage reaches under with his left hand and applies sankyo until uke raises to his toes. Nage then cuts straight down. Nage pins uke by stepping in with his left leg and turns his body to the right. This increases the torque on uke's wrist.

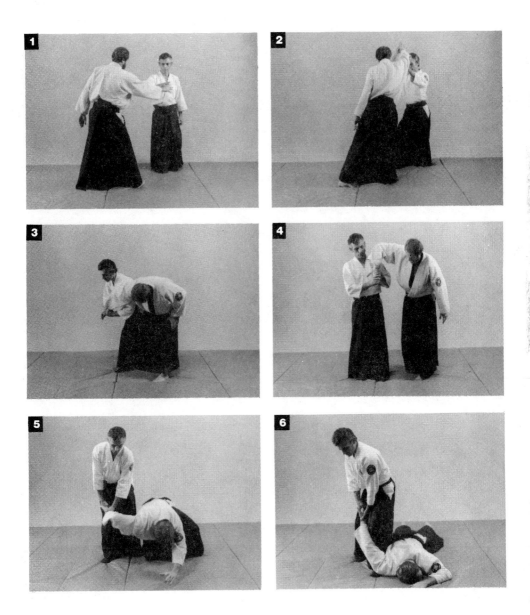

Kata Tori Kotegaeshi. Uke grabs nage with one hand on the lapel. Nage reaches up and places his right hand on top and the left hand on the bottom of uke's hand. From this position, nage steps to the outside and applies kotegaeshi (wrist turn-out). Note that the entire body is used to apply the technique.

Kata Tori Kokyunage. As uke steps in and grabs nage's lapel, nage grabs the gi and applies weight underside. Nage then steps back, breaking uke's balance, and applies downward pressure on uke's elbow.

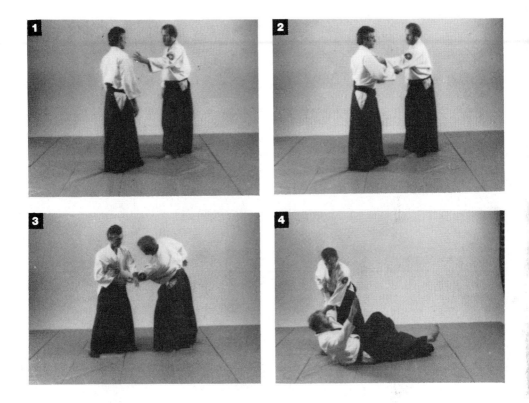

Kata Tori Kokyunage. In this technique, uke grabs nage and pulls him in. Nage traps uke's hand with his right hand and grabs his elbow with the left hand. Nage steps forward, taking a bow, while lifting up on uke's elbow.

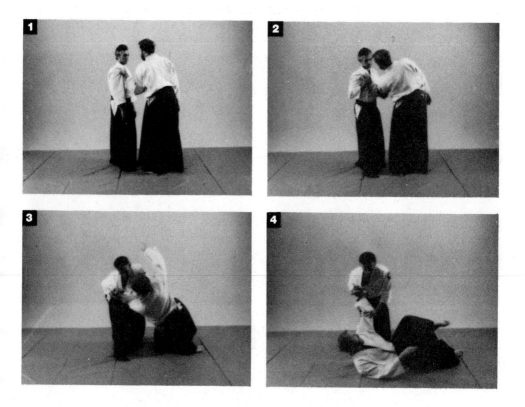

Katate — Wrist Grab

Katate Tori Nikkyo — Same side. Uke grabs nage's left hand with his right hand. Nage steps off the line of attack and lightly traps uke's hand with his right hand. At the same time, nage circles the fingertips of his left hand to the outside of uke's grab. From here, nage moves the left hand over uke's wrist and extends ki down toward uke's one-point. Do not press down on uke's wrist, but try to let your fingers go over the wrist and down. After uke has gone down to his knees, apply ikkyo to finish the technique.

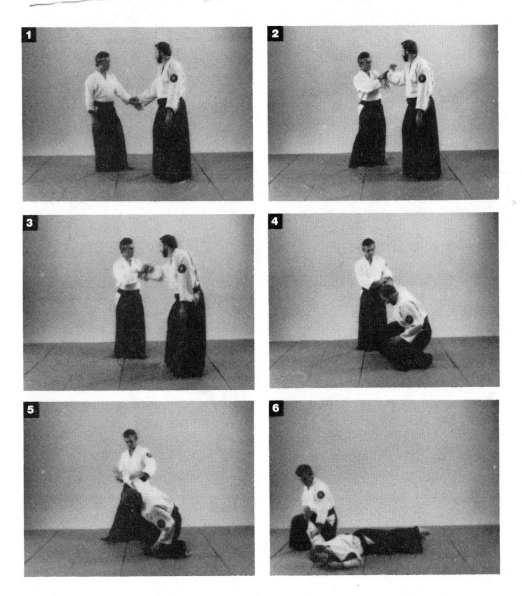

Katate Tori Nikkyo — Opposite side. Uke grabs nage's right hand with his right hand. The technique is applied as in the previous nikkyo. Step to the side and apply nikkyo.

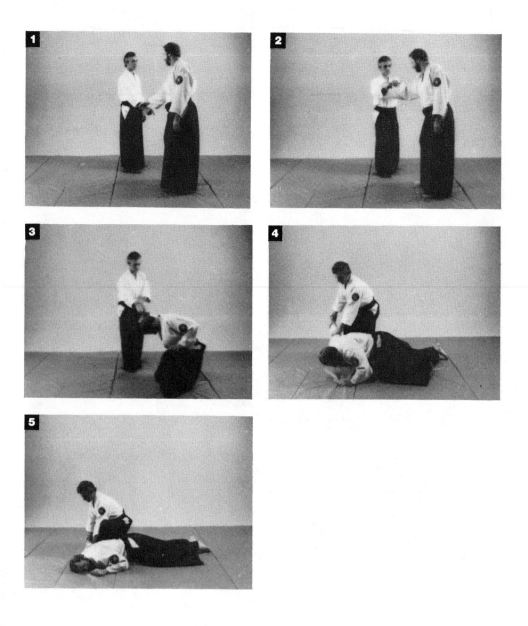

Katate Tori Nikkyo — Rear grab. Uke grabs nage's right wrist with his right hand. Nage pivots and applies nikkyo.

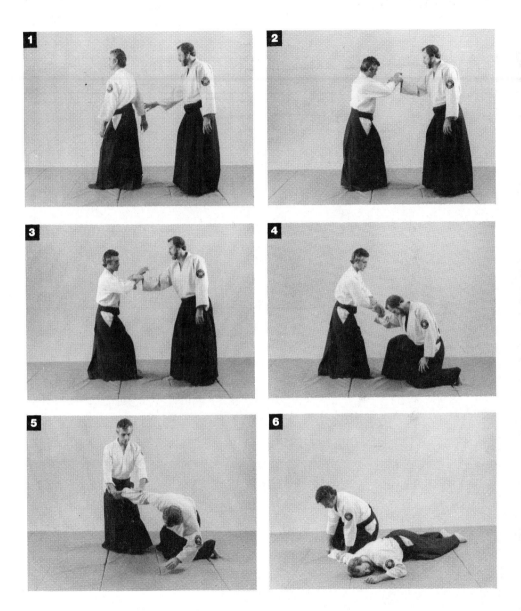

Katate Tori Nikkyo — Side grab. Uke grabs nage's left wrist with his right hand. Nage traps uke's hand with his right hand and rolls his elbow over and down on uke's forearm.

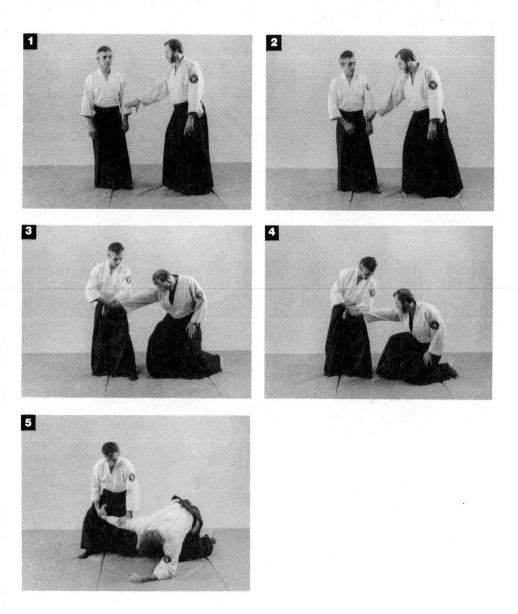

Katate Tori Ikkyo. From a right ai-hanmi stance, uke grabs nage's right wrist with his right hand. Nage slides forward with his right foot and makes a large circle with his right arm as the left hand comes under uke's elbow. Nage steps through with the left leg and extends down. Note that nage's hips are directly over uke's elbow.

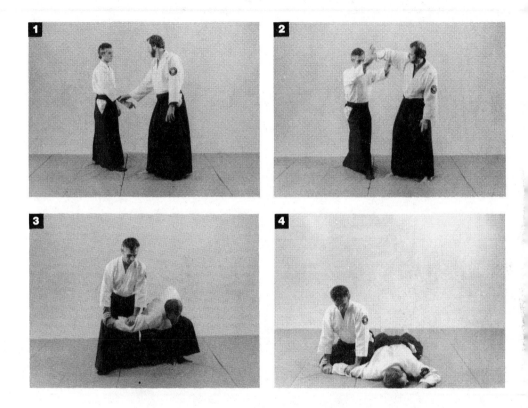

Katate Tori Kokyunage. Both partners start in right hanmi. Uke grabs nage's right wrist with his right hand. Nage leaps behind uke and leads his energy down and to the side. The movement is the same as in choyaku undo. Nage brings his left arm over uke's left shoulder and applies weight underside. Nage reverses his direction and brings his right arm in front of uke's face and down over the left shoulder. To finish the movement nage steps through with his right leg.

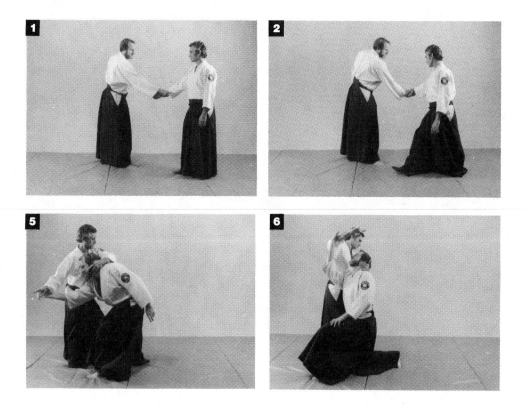

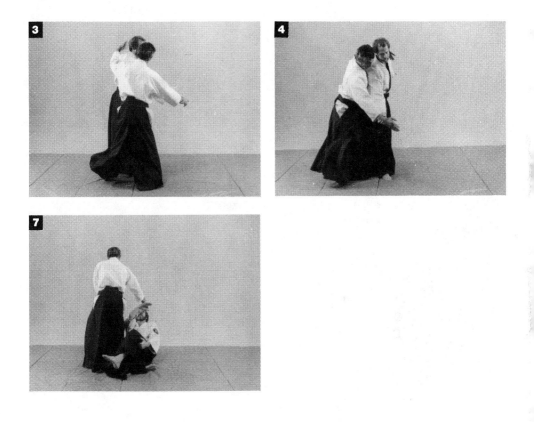

Katate Tori Kokyunage. The initial movement of this technique is the same as the previous technique. After nage jumps behind uke, his left arm extends down on uke's elbow. To finish the technique, nage continues to turn and extend down. The pin is done by holding the elbow in place while nage pulls the elbow back and to the side.

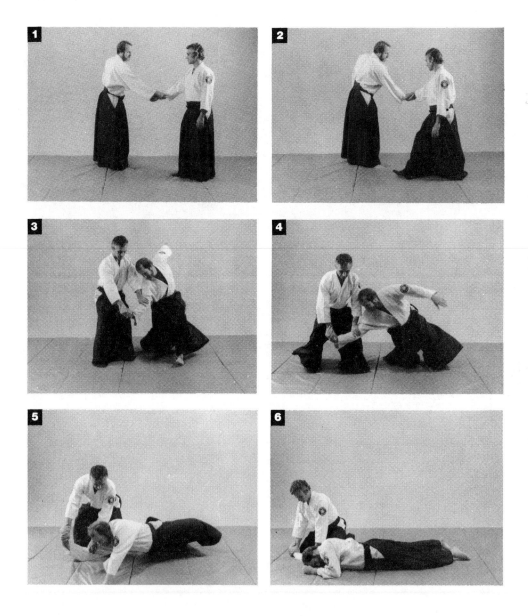

Katate Tori Kaitenage. This technique starts from gyaku-hanmi. Nage slides forward with his right foot and extends ki out his fingertips. Nage's left hand comes up into uke's face. This movement can be a strike or merely an attempt to surprise (lead uke's mind) by faking a blow. Nage steps under uke's arm and pivots. At this point nage drops his arm and steps to uke's right side. This action turns uke and leads his body forward. Nage grabs uke's wrist and continues uke's arm in a "wheel-like" pattern.

Katate Tori Kokyunage. From a left ai-hanmi, nage slides in with his left foot and extends his ki up and across toward uke's right shoulder. Nage reaches up with his right hand and grabs uke's shoulder, neck or chin. Nage continues his movement by curling around uke. The technique is completed by pulling down slightly on uke's neck or shoulder and pointing the left arm over the shoulder and down.

Ryote Tori — Two-Hand Grab

Ryote Tori Tenchinage. Starting from a left ai-hanmi, nage slides forward and extends down and back with this left hand. Simultaneously, nage brings up his right hand toward uke's face with his palm facing up. Nage steps through with the right leg, turns his right hand palm down and points his fingers toward the ground.

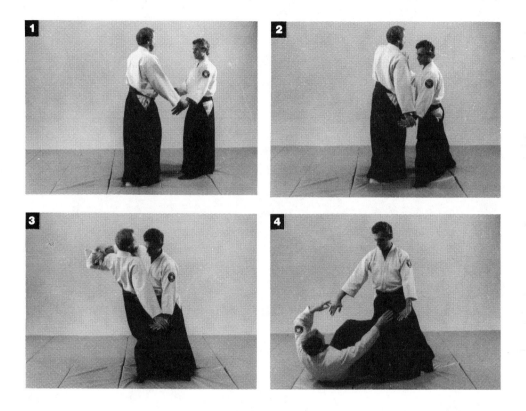

Ryote Tori Shihonage. Nage glides in front and across uke's body, bringing his left shoulder to uke's right shoulder. As nage glides in, he extends forward and then up, turning under uke's outstretched arms. After completing his turn, nage extends straight down in a cutting action.

Ryote Tori Kokyunage. From left ai-hanmi, nage steps back with his right foot which pulls uke's arms straight and draws him forward. As uke's momentum continues forward, nage drops down and leads uke over his right shoulder. Note that nage's arms drop and then circle forward.

Ryote Mochi Zenponage. Starting in left ai-hanmi, nage glides in and across, bringing his right shoulder to uke's left shoulder. Notice the extension of nage's right arm under uke's left arm. Nage rotates uke's left palm up and brings it down toward his one-point. With uke's arm locked in this position, nage steps through with his back leg and slightly twists his hips.

Ryote Mochi Nikkyo. From right ai-hanmi, nage steps to uke's right and snakes his hand to the outside of uke's wrist. Nage points his fingers over uke's wrist and toward his one-point. Nage finishes the technique by applying ikkyo.

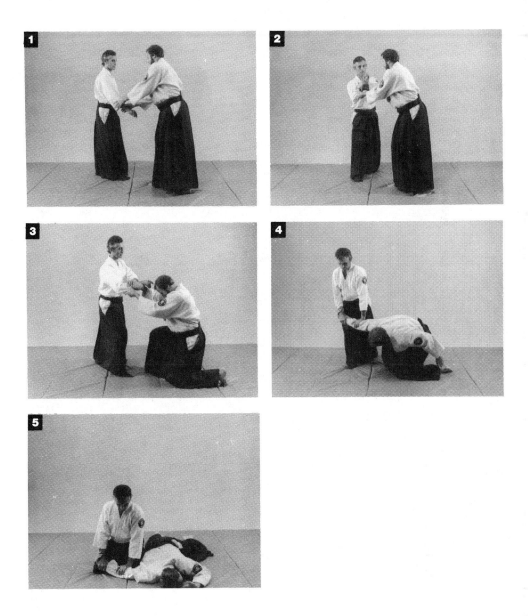

Ryote Mochi Sayunage. In left hanmi, nage bends his elbow and drops his center of gravity. He slides in with his left foot and extends his left arm across uke's face and shoulder. Nage uses an atemi (strike) to the solar plexus and continues to move forward.

Ryote Mochi Ikkyo. In right hanmi, nage again drops his center and bends his elbow. He then comes up with the entire body making a large circle with his right arm. Nage's left arm comes under the uke's elbow and pushes toward uke's face. Nage steps through with the left leg and immediately extends down.

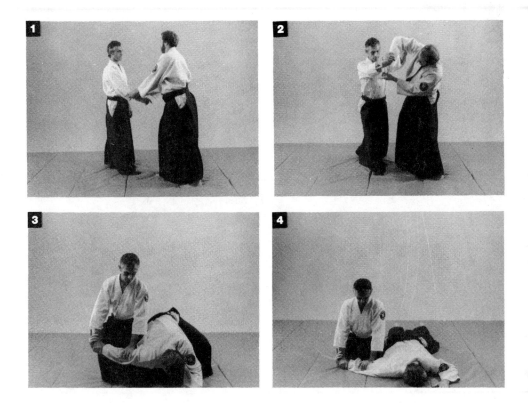

Ushiro — Grabs From Behind

Ushiro Tori Zeponage. Starting with uke and nage both in left hanmi, nage turns his palms up, bends his elbows, and extends forward. Nage steps forward and twists his hips. It is important to step in front of the back leg so that uke has room to clear nage's hips and tumble properly.

Ushiro Tori Kokyunage. Nage steps back at an angle with his left foot and follows through with his right foot. Note the extension of nage's arms. He then lifts up uke's knees and continues the backward motion of his body. Notice that the hips have also rotated.

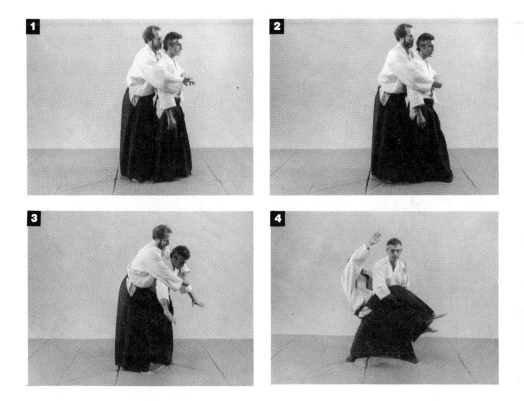

Ushiro Tekubi Tori Kotegaeshi. Nage steps forward with his left foot as he simultaneously grabs uke's left wrist with his right hand. Nage then pivots with his entire body on his left leg and steps back with his right leg which breaks uke's grip. From this position, nage applies kotegaeshi.

Ushiro Tekubi Tori Ikkyo. Nage steps back and to the side of uke as his hands lead up from the fingertips. Nage steps through with his left leg and drops his arms. As uke's grip becomes weak, nage releases his left hand and extends down on uke's elbow. Nage's right hand circles in toward his body and over uke's wrist. This is done after nage has uke's elbow under control. Notice that nage merely pushes uke forward. If there is more than one attacker, you cannot use a pin. You must be free to move.

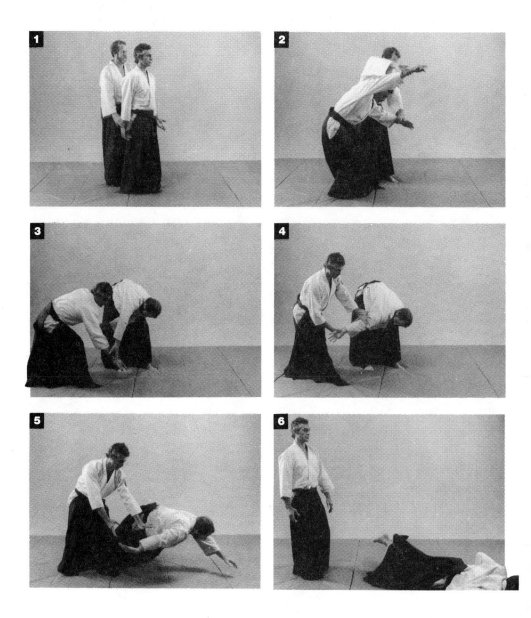

Ushiro Tekubi Tori Sayunage. Nage steps to the side with his left foot. Nage then steps through and back while raising his right arm across uke's neck. Nage continues moving his one-point back while applying weight underside.

Ushiro Tekubi Tori Kokyunage. Nage pivots to the left and raises his right arm from the fingertips. The left arm remains down. Nage continues to turn and then steps with his right foot. Nage's right arm extends out and the left arm extends down and away from uke's body.

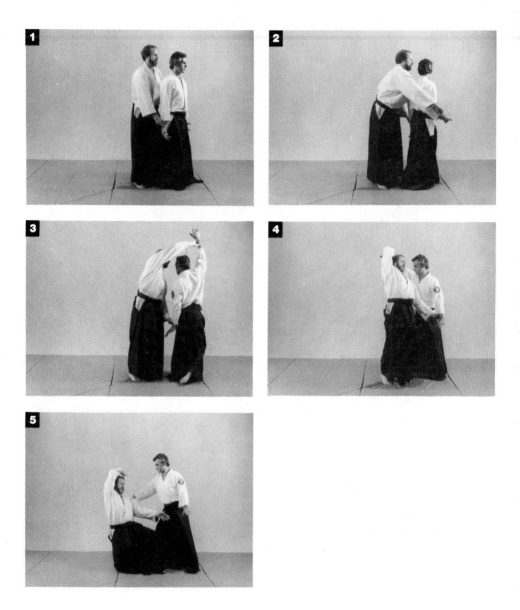

Kata Tori Shomenuchi

Kata Tori Shomenuchi Ikkyo. Uke grabs nage's left shoulder. Uke steps forward and strikes shomen. Nage catches uke's arm under the elbow and the wrist. He punches uke's elbow toward his face and turns his body around. Nage steps through with his right leg and extends down.

Kata Tori Shomenuchi Kokyunage. From a lapel grab, uke steps in and strikes shomen. Nage pivots to his left and protects his head with his right hand. Nage allows uke's strike to continue while he drops to his left knee and takes a bow. Notice in picture 3 that nage's right hand has trapped uke's hand while the left arm is extended under the armpit. In this position uke is locked in and must tumble when nage bows.

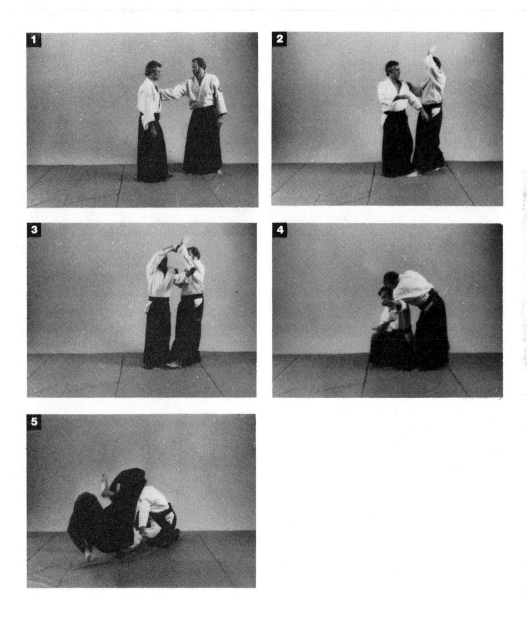

Kata Tori Shomenuchi Zenponage. Nage turns to the left to avoid the shomen strike. As the strike comes down, nage extends the right arm under uke's armpit and traps the wrist with the left hand. Nage steps forward and throws in the direction of uke's weak balance points.

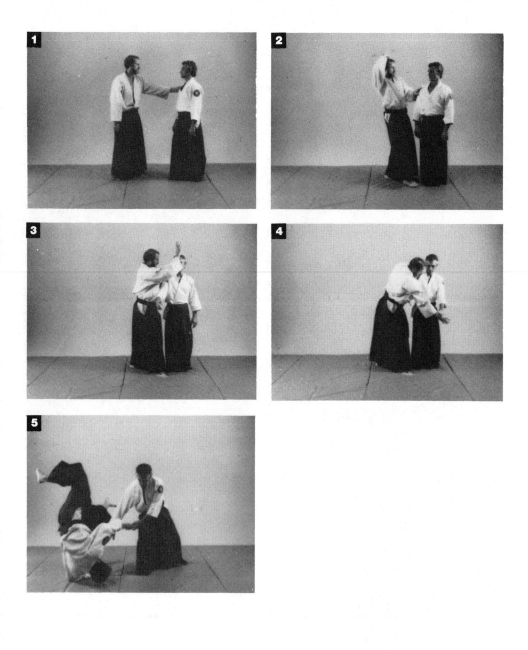

Punches — Kicks

Katate Tori Munetsuki Tenchinage. Uke attempts a punch to the face as he holds nage's wrist. Nage slides to the inside protecting his face while extending back and down with the right hand. As nage steps through with the left foot, the left hand turns over and energy is extended down over the shoulder. Note the proper throwing angle.

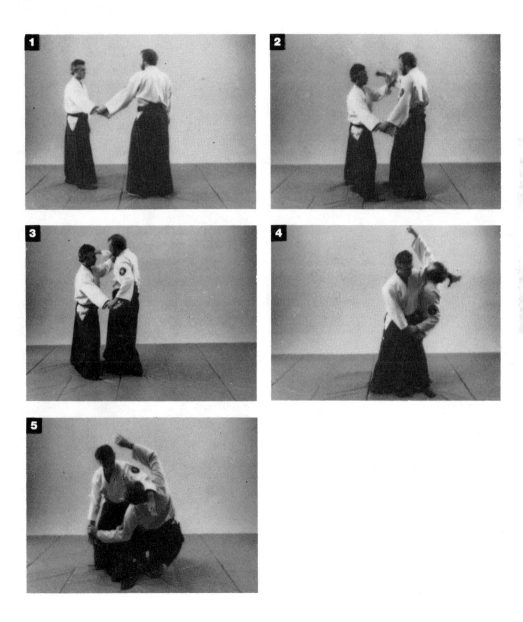

Hook Punch — Backfist. As uke delivers a hook punch to nage's head, nage slips the punch and moves behind the uke. Uke continues the attack by following with a backfist which is again aimed at nage's head. Nage continues to move in a circle behind uke while applying weight to the fist and elbow.

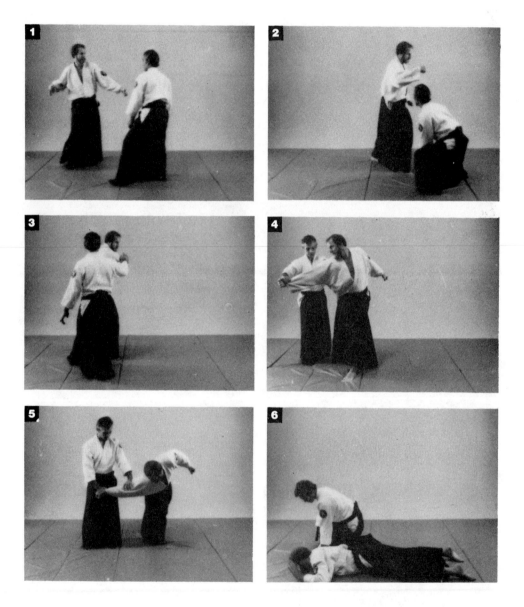

Round Kick. Pictures 1 and 2 demonstrate a back leg round kick. As uke attempts the kick, nage slides in before uke can extend the kick from the knee (fold position). Nage continues to move forward and can easily throw uke because his weight is supported on one leg.

Front Thrust Kick. The first three pictures demonstrate proper attack by uke of the front thrust kick. As uke attempts to strike nage with the right leg front kick, nage moves to the side and places the right hand under the knee and the left hand on uke's chest. Nage then continues to move forward as he lifts up on the kicking leg, causing uke to lose balance.

Turning Back Kick. Uke's proper attack is shown in pictures 1, 2, 3 and 4. To defend against this kick, nage slides to the side and in. From this position, nage grabs uke's shoulders and applies weight underside down and back. Note that nage turns his hips and uses the one-point to do the throw.

GLOSSARY

Ai Harmony, blend, oneness

Aiki Harmony with the universe

Aikido The way of life through harmony with the universe; a non-violent art of self-defense

Aiki-Taiso Exercises derived from the self-defense movements of aikido

Atemi Strike; a blow to the vital parts of the body to stun the opponent

Bo Wooden staff or rod

Bokken Wooden sword

Bu Martial

Budo The way of life through application of the principles of martial arts

Bushido Warrior's code; the way of the warrior

Dan Black-belt rank

Do Path, road, a way of life

Dojo Training hall; place of enlightenment

Gi Training uniform

Hakama Long skirtlike formal wear; normally worn by advanced aikido students

Hanmi Ready stance with either left or right foot forward

Hantai Opposite

Hara Center of gravity of a person; area below the navel. It is the reservoir of ki.

Hidari Left (direction)

Hiji Elbow

Hiji-otoshi Dropping the opponent's elbow to lead his fall

Ikkyo A method of controlling an opponent by cranking the arm and applying pressure to the elbow

Irimi Entering technique without collision

Jo   Staff approximately 50 inches long

Jo-kata (Jogi)   Techniques to throw the opponent with jo

Jo-tori   Disarming jo attack

Kaiten   To turn like a wheel

Kaiten-nage   Windmill throw

Kamae   Ready stance

Kata   From practice of pre-arranged exercise; also, the shoulder

Kata Tori   Shoulder grab

Katate Tori   Wrist grab

Katate Tori ryote mochi   Two hands grabbing one wrist

Ken   Sword

Ki   The essence of the universe; the source of energy of nature; the power of one's mind

Kiai   To shout with ki; to alarm or frighten your opponent

Koho   To the rear

Koho Tento undo   Backward roll

Kokyu   Breathing; the rhythm of ki movement

Kokyudosa   Special exercises of extension

Kokyunage   Breath or timing throw

Kosa   To cross or intersect

Kotai   To move backward

Kotegaeshi   Wrist turn-out; reverse wrist throw

Kotegaeshi undo   Wrist turn-out exercise. Strengthens and limbers the wrist

Kyu   Ranks before black belt

Ma-ai   Proper distance between opponents

Misogi or ki breathing   Breathing exercise to unify mind and body

Munetsuki   Punch to chest area

Nage   The person who is attacked

Nikkyo   Wrist-bending technique

One-point   Hara; center of gravity of one's body

O-sensei   Founder of Aikido — Morihei Ueshiba, 1883-1969

Randori   Freestyle exercise of attack

Ryote Tori   Holding both wrists

Ryote mochi   Holding with both hands

Sankyo   Wrist-twisting technique

Sankyo-undo   Exercise to twist wrist around the vertical axis

Sayu   Left and right

Seiza   Formal Japanese posture; kneeling position with back straight

Shihonage   Four-direction throw

Shodo-o-seizu   To control the first move

Shomenuchi   Blow to the forehead from above

Taiso (undo)   Exercise

Tanto   Knife or dagger

Tekubi (kote)   Wrist

Tekubi kosa-undo   Wrist-crossing exercise

Tenchinage   Heaven and earth throw. One hand points up, the other down.

Tenkan   Turning; rotating about a vertical axis

Tori (dori)   To grab

Udefuri undo   Exercise: swinging arms from side to side while keeping the body still

Udefuri choyaku undo   Exercise: turning 180 degrees. Arms swing away from body during the turn

Uke   The attacker who gets thrown by the nage

Ukemi   Roll or fall taken by the uke when thrown

Ushiro   Back or behind

Ushiro Kubishimi   Rear choke

Waza   Technique or art

Yokomen   Side of the head

Yokomenuchi   Strike to the side of the head

About the Authors

Bill Sosa has had some other martial arts training in his background, but at the age of 31, he encountered a unique martial art — aikido — which proved to be a dramatic turning point in his life. Ever since, he has been fascinated with aikido's approach, one that can be utilized in everyday life. He found the principal aim was the personal growth and development of the physical and spiritual. In essence, it is a "life of learning" that he takes very seriously. The author has been practicing aikido now for the past 20 years and holds the rank of godan. For the past 12 years he has been the Chief Instructor at the Southwestern Aikido Institute in Dallas, Texas. He spends most of his time teaching aikido and travels throughout the year holding seminars.

Bryan Robbins began his practice of the martial arts in 1970 with the study of tae kwon do (Korean karate). He presently holds the rank of fourth-degree black belt. Robbins started his study of aikido in 1981 and obtained his black belt in May, 1985. He is now a second-degree black belt in aikido. He is currently an assistant professor of physical education at Southern Methodist University (SMU) in Dallas, Texas. In 1971 he started teaching karate as a physical education class at SMU with his karate instructor, Keith Yates. In 1983, Sosa and Robbins started teaching aikido at a university class at SMU. In addition to his work in the martial arts, Robbins was named one of the diving coaches of the United States 1975 and 1979 Pan American Games and the 1976 and 1980 Olympic Games. He graduated from SMU in 1968 with a B.A. degree and received his M. Ed. from the University of Arkansas in 1971. In 1975, Robbins married Laura Powers. They have four children — Melissa, Andrew, Matthew and Jennifer.

UNIQUE LITERARY BOOKS OF THE WORLD

Also publishers of:
Inside Karate
Inside Kung-Fu

UNIQUE PUBLICATIONS
4201 Vanowen Place
Burbank, CA 91505

PLEASE WRITE IN
FOR OUR LATEST CATALOG